The Batsford Book of
Light Verse for Children

A thousand guilders! The Mayor looked blue

The Batsford Book of
Light Verse
for Children

Edited by Gavin Ewart
Nicolas Bentley drew the pictures

B.T. BATSFORD LTD · LONDON

For Jane and Julian
(children of the Fifties)

ISBN 0 7134 0916 9

First published 1978
Selection copyright 1978 Gavin Ewart
Set in 11 on 12 pt Monophoto Plantin by Keyspools Ltd, Golborne,
Lancashire
Printed and bound in Great Britain by Butler & Tanner Ltd, Frome
for the publishers B. T. Batsford Ltd,
4 Fitzhardinge Street, London W1H 0AH

Contents

Acknowledgements

The Editor and Publishers would like to thank the following for permission to reproduce poems that are in copyright:

Hilaire Belloc, *Jim*, *The Python*, *The Frog*, *The Crocodile*, *The Hippopotamus* (from THE BAD CHILD'S BOOK OF BEASTS, TOGETHER WITH MORE BEASTS FOR WORSE CHILDREN AND CAUTIONARY TALES): Duckworth and Co., London

Alan Brownjohn, *Parrot* and *Elephant* (from BROWNJOHN'S BEASTS): Macmillan, London and Basingstoke

Noel Coward, *Any Part of Piggy* (from NOT YET THE DODO): Heinemann, London

Walter de la Mare, *The Huntsman*, *Pooh!*, *Miss T.*, *Hi!* (from A CHOICE OF WALTER DE LA MARE'S VERSE, edited by W. H. Auden): Faber and Faber Limited, London

Lord Alfred Douglas, *The Ferret*, *The Ostrich*, *The Weasel*: Edward Colman, Literary Executor of Lord Alfred Douglas

Gavin Ewart, *The Weather*: the Author

Robert Graves, *George II and the Chinese Emperor* (from ANN AT HIGHWOOD HALL): Cassell and Company, London

Roy Fuller, *Leaving School* (from POOR ROY): André Deutsch, London

Maurice Hare, *Byways in Biography* (from THE WEEK-END BOOK): The Nonesuch Press, London

Ted Hughes, *Leaves* (from SEASON SONGS): Faber and Faber Limited, London

Phyllis McGinley, *Trial and Error* (from *The New Yorker*) included in THE WEEK-END BOOK: The Nonesuch Press, London

A. A. Milne, *Bad Sir Brian Botany* (from WHEN WE WERE VERY YOUNG): Methuen and Company, London

Mervyn Peake, *The Frivolous Cake* (from TITUS GROAN): Mrs Maeve Peake

Stevie Smith, *The Jungle Husband* (from COLLECTED POEMS OF STEVIE SMITH): Allen Lane, London

Marie de L. Welch, *The Ibis* (from THE WEEK-END BOOK): The Nonesuch Press, London

Introduction

Light verse is notoriously hard to define. It can be serious, in its criticism of life (like Byron's *Don Juan*, the poetry of Clough, and Pope's *The Rape Of The Lock*—the supreme example). Yet it never deals in strong emotion; above all, it is never solemn or sad. It may be humorous, or partly humorous. It can be bitter. It can be purely lyrical. A good many songs are included in this collection.

Light verse for children? All nursery rhymes come into this category, puzzles, riddles, tongue-twisters. Almost every one of the traditional poems here, of this kind, comes from Iona and Peter Opie's *Oxford Nursery Rhyme Book*, a collection so complete, well organized and interesting, that it is impossible to by-pass it.

It is obvious that some of the poems included are beyond the intellectual grasp of very young children. My notes are supposed to help—but explanations are no substitute for personal experience. Herrick's wine and women may seem out of place (and *A Ring Presented To Julia* contains a complicated 'metaphysical' conceit into the bargain) but a 17-year-old would have some idea of what he was on about. Hood's puns sometimes need explaining; but Hood, of his kind, is such a good poet and so neglected by school anthologies, that he seemed a worthy candidate.

It is always worth rescuing old poems. Browning's *The Pied Piper Of Hamelin*, probably the longest piece of light verse ever written specifically for children, is not now as well-known as it used to be. The same could probably be said of Cowper's *John Gilpin*. To lose the past, and the sense of the past, is always a bad thing.

I owe a debt of gratitude to my friend Sam Carr, who drew my attention to the animal poems of Lord Alfred Douglas.

My advice to children let loose on this book is: try the short ones first. If you like them, go on to the longer poems. My advice to grown-up readers-aloud is the same. But try

The Pied Piper. It's a wonderful performance piece. In fact, it's foolproof. And it doesn't matter if the kids don't understand every word.

1. STORIES

The Pied Piper of Hamelin

I

Hamelin Town's in Brunswick,
By famous Hanover city;
  The river Weser, deep and wide,
  Washes its wall on the southern side;
  A pleasanter spot you never spied;
But, when begins my ditty,
  Almost five hundred years ago,
  To see the townsfolk suffer so
    From vermin, was a pity.

II

Rats!
They fought the dogs and killed the cats,
  And bit the babies in the cradles,
And ate the cheeses out of the vats.
  And licked the soup from the cooks' own ladles,
Split open the kegs of salted sprats,
Made nests inside men's Sunday hats,
And even spoiled the women's chats,
  By drowning their speaking
  With shrieking and squeaking
In fifty different sharps and flats.

III

At last the people in a body
  To the Town Hall came flocking:
'Tis clear,' cried they, 'our Mayor's a noddy;
  'And as for our Corporation—shocking!
'To think we buy gowns lined with ermine
'For dolts that can't or won't determine
'What's best to rid us of our vermin!
'You hope, because you're old and obese,
'To find in the furry civic robe ease?
'Rouse up, sirs! Give your brains a racking
'To find the remedy we're lacking,
'Or, sure as fate, we'll send you packing!'

13

At this the Mayor and Corporation
Quaked with a mighty consternation.

IV

An hour they sate in council,
   At length the Mayor broke silence:
'For a guilder I'd my ermine gown sell;
   'I wish I were a mile hence!
'It's easy to bid one rack one's brain—
'I'm sure my poor head aches again,
'I've scratched it so, and all in vain.
'Oh for a trap, a trap, a trap!'
Just as he said this, what should hap
At the chamber door but a gentle tap?
'Bless us,' cried the Mayor, 'what's that?'
(With the Corporation as he sat,
Looking little though wondrous fat;
Nor brighter was his eye, nor moister
Than a too-long-opened oyster,
Save when at noon his paunch grew mutinous
For a plate of turtle green and glutinous)
'Only a scraping of shoes on the mat?
'Anything like the sound of a rat
'Makes my heart go pit-a-pat!'

V

'Come in!'—the Mayor cried, looking bigger:
And in did come the strangest figure!
His queer long coat from heel to head
Was half of yellow and half of red,
And he himself was tall and thin,
With sharp blue eyes, each like a pin,
And light loose hair, yet swarthy skin,
No tuft on cheek nor beard on chin,
But lips where smiles went out and in;
There was no guessing his kith and kin;
And nobody could enough admire
The tall man and his quaint attire.
Quoth one: 'It's as if my great-grandsire,
'Starting up at the Trump of Doom's tone,
'Had walked this way from his painted tombstone!'

14

VI

He advanced to the council-table:
And, 'Please your honours,' said he, 'I'm able,
'By means of a secret charm, to draw
'All creatures living beneath the sun,
'That creep or swim or fly or run,
'After me so as you never saw!
'And I chiefly use my charm
'On creatures that do people harm,
'The mole and toad and newt and viper;
'And people call me the Pied Piper.'
(And here they noticed round his neck
A scarf of red and yellow stripe,
To match with his coat of the self-same cheque;
And at the scarf's end hung a pipe;
And his fingers they noticed were ever straying
As if impatient to be playing
Upon his pipe, as low it dangled
Over his vesture so old-fangled.)
'Yet,' said he, 'poor Piper as I am,
'In Tartary I freed the Cham,
'Last June, from his huge swarms of gnats,
'I eased in Asia the Nizam
'Of a montrous brood of vampyre-bats:
'And as for what your brain bewilders,
'If I can rid your town of rats
'Will you give me a thousand guilders?'
'One? fifty thousand!'—was the exclamation
Of the astonished Mayor and Corporation.

VII

Into the street the Piper stept,
　Smiling first a little smile,
As if he knew what magic slept
　In his quiet pipe the while;
Then, like a musical adept,
To blow the pipe his lips he wrinkled,
And green and blue his sharp eyes twinkled,
Like a candle-flame where salt is sprinkled;
And ere three shrill notes the pipe uttered,
You heard as though an army muttered;

And the muttering grew to a grumbling;
And the grumbling grew to a mighty rumbling;
And out of the houses the rats came tumbling.
Great rats, small rats, lean rats, brawny rats,
Brown rats, black rats, grey rats, tawny rats,
Grave old plodders, gay young friskers,
 Fathers, mothers, uncles, cousins,
Cocking tails and pricking whiskers,
 Families by tens and dozens,
Brothers, sisters, husbands, wives—
Followed the Piper for their lives.
From street to street he piped advancing,
And step for step they followed dancing,
Until they came to the river Weser
Wherein all plunged and perished!
—Save one who, stout as Julius Caesar,
Swam across and lived to carry
(As he, the manuscript he cherished)
To Rat-land home his commentary:
Which was, 'At the first shrill notes of the pipe
'I heard a sound as of scraping tripe,
'And putting apples, wondrous ripe,
'Into a cider-press's gripe:
'And moving away of pickle-tub-boards,
'And leaving ajar of conserve-cupboards,
'And a drawing the corks of train-oil-flasks,
'And a breaking the hoops of butter-casks:
'And it seemed as if a voice
'(Sweeter far than by harp or psaltery
'Is breathed) called out, "Oh rats, rejoice!
' "The world is grown to one vast drysaltery!
' "So munch on, crunch on, take your nuncheon,
' "Breakfast, supper, dinner, luncheon!"
'And just as a bulky sugar-puncheon,
'All ready staved, like a great sun shone
'Glorious scarce an inch before me,
'Just as methought it said, "Come, bore me!"
'—I found the Weser rolling o'er me.'

VIII

You should have heard the Hamelin people
Ringing the bells till they rocked the steeple!
'Go!' cried the Mayor, 'and get long poles,
'Poke out the nests and block up the holes!
'Consult with carpenters and builders,
'And leave in our town not even a trace
'Of the rats!'—when suddenly, up the face
Of the Piper perked in the market-place,
With a, 'First, if you please, my thousand guilders!'

IX

A thousand guilders! The Mayor looked blue;
So did the Corporation too.
For council dinners made rare havoc
With Claret, Moselle, Vin-de-Grave, Hock;
And half the money would replenish
Their cellar's biggest butt with Rhenish.
To pay this sum to a wandering fellow
With a gipsy coat of red and yellow!
'Beside,' quoth the Mayor with a knowing wink,
'Our business was done at the river's brink;
'We saw with our eyes the vermin sink,
'And what's dead can't come to life, I think.
'So, friend, we're not the folks to shrink
'From the duty of giving you something to drink,
'And a matter of money to put in your poke;
'But as for the guilders, what we spoke
'Of them, as you very well know, was in joke.
'Beside, our losses have made us thrifty.
'A thousand guilders! Come, take fifty!'

X

The Piper's face fell, and he cried,
'No trifling! I can't wait, beside!
'I've promised to visit by dinner-time
'Bagdad, and accept the prime
'Of the Head-Cook's pottage, all he's rich in,
'For having left, in the Caliph's kitchen,
'Of a nest of scorpions no survivor:
'With him I proved no bargain-driver,

17

'With you, don't think I'll bate a stiver!
'And folks who put me in a passion
'May find me pipe after another fashion.'

XI

'How?' cried the Mayor, 'd'ye think I brook
'Being worse treated than a Cook?
'Insulted by a lazy ribald
'With idle pipe and vesture piebald?
'You threaten us, fellow? Do your worst,
'Blow your pipe there till you burst!'

XII

Once more he stept into the street.
    And to his lips again
Laid his long pipe of smooth straight cane;
And ere he blew three notes (such sweet
Soft notes as yet musician's cunning
    Never gave the enraptured air)
There was a rustling, that seemed like a bustling
Of merry crowds justling at pitching and hustling,
Small feet were pattering, wooden shoes clattering,
Little hands clapping and little tongues chattering,
And, like fowls in a farm-yard when barley is scattering,
    Out came the children running.
    All the little boys and girls,
    With rosy cheeks and flaxen curls,
    And sparkling eyes and teeth like pearls,
    Tripping and skipping, ran merrily after
    The wonderful music with shouting and laughter.

XIII

The Mayor was dumb, and the Council stood
As if they were changed into blocks of wood,
Unable to move a step, or cry
To the children merrily skipping by.
—Could only follow with the eye
That joyous crowd at the Piper's back.
But how the Mayor was on the rack,
And the wretched Council's bosoms beat,
As the Piper turned from the High Street

18

To where the Weser rolled its waters
Right in the way of their sons and daughters!
However he turned from South to West,
And to Koppelberg Hill his steps addressed,
And after him the children pressed;
Great was the joy in every breast.
'He never can cross that mighty top!
'He's forced to let the piping drop,
'And we shall see our children stop!'
When, lo, as they reached the mountain-side,
A wondrous portal opened wide,
As if a cavern was suddenly hollowed;
And the Piper advanced and the children followed.
And when all were in to the very last,
The door in the mountain-side shut fast.
Did I say, all? No! One was lame,
And could not dance the whole of the way;
And in after years, if you would blame
His sadness, he was used to say,—
'It's dull in our town since my playmates left!
'I can't forget that I'm bereft
'Of all the pleasant sights they see,
'Which the Piper also promised me.
'For he led us, he said, to a joyous land,
'Joining the town and just at hand,
'Where waters gushed and fruit-trees grew.
'And flowers put forth a fairer hue,
'And everything was strange and new;
'The sparrows were brighter than peacocks here,
'And their dogs outran our fallow deer,
'And honey-bees had lost their stings,
'And horses were born with eagles' wings:
'And just as I became assured
'My lame foot would be speedily cured,
'The music stopped and I stood still,
'And found myself outside the hill,
'Left alone against my will,
'To go now limping as before,
'And never hear of that country more!'

19

XIV
Alas, alas for Hamelin!

There came into many a burgher's pate
A text which says that Heaven's gate
Opes to the rich at as easy a rate
As the needle's eye takes a camel in!
The Mayor sent East, West, North, and South,
To offer the Piper, by word of mouth,
    Wherever it was men's lot to find him,
Silver and gold to his heart's content,
If he'd only return the way he went,
    And bring the children behind him.
But when they saw 'twas a lost endeavour,
And Piper and dancers were gone for ever,
They made a decree that lawyers never
    Should think their records dated duly
If, after the day of the month and year,
These words did not as well appear,
'And so long after what happened here
    'On the Twenty-second of July,
'Thirteen hundred and seventy-six:'
And the better in memory to fix
The place of the children's last retreat,
They called it, the Pied Piper's Street—
Where any one playing on pipe or tabor,
Was sure for the future to lose his labour.
Nor suffered they hostelry or tavern
    To shock with mirth a street so solemn;
But opposite the place of the cavern
    They wrote the story on a column,
And on the great church-window painted
The same, to make the world acquainted
How their children were stolen away,
And there it stands to this very day.
And I must not omit to say
That in Transylvania there's a tribe
Of alien people that ascribe
The outlandish ways and dress
On which their neighbours lay such stress,
To their fathers and mothers having risen

Out of some subterranean prison
Into which they were trepanned
Long ago in a mighty band
Out of Hamelin town in Brunswick land,
But how or why, they don't understand.

XV

So, Willy, let me and you be wipers
Of scores out with all men—especially pipers!
And, whether they pipe us free from rats or from mice,
If we've promised them aught, let us keep our promise!

ROBERT BROWNING

Faithless Sally Brown

An Old Ballad

Young Ben he was a nice young man,
   A carpenter by trade;
And he fell in love with Sally Brown,
   That was a lady's maid.

But as they fetched a walk one day,
   They met a pressgang crew;
And Sally she did faint away,
   Whilst Ben he was brought to.

The Boatswain swore with wicked words,
   Enough to shock a saint,
That though she did seem in a fit,
   'Twas nothing but a feint.

'Come, girl,' said he, 'hold up your head,
   He'll be as good as me;
For when your swain is in our boat,
   A boatswain he will be.'

So when they'd made their game of her,
   And taken off her elf,
She roused, and found she only was
   A coming to herself.

'And is he gone, and is he gone?'
   She cried, and wept outright:
'Then I will to the water side,
   And see him out of sight.'

A waterman came up to her,
   'Now, young woman,' said he,
'If you weep on so, you will make
   Eye-water in the sea.'

'Alas! they've taken my beau Ben
   To sail with old Benbow';
And her woe began to run afresh,
   As if she'd said 'Gee woe'!

Says he, 'They've only taken him
    To the Tender ship, you see';
'The Tender ship,' cried Sally Brown,
    'What a hard-ship that must be!

'Oh! would I were a mermaid now,
    For then I'd follow him;
But oh!—I'm not a fish-woman,
    And so I cannot swim.

'Alas! I was not born beneath
    The Virgin and the Scales,
So I must curse my cruel stars,
    And walk about in Wales.'

Now Ben had sailed to many a place
    That's underneath the world;
But in two years the ship came home,
    And all her sails were furled.

But when he called on Sally Brown,
    To see how she went on,
He found she'd got another Ben,
    Whose Christian name was John.

'O Sally Brown, O Sally Brown,
    How could you serve me so?
I've met with many a breeze before,
    But never such a blow.'

Then reading on his 'bacco box,
    He heaved a bitter sigh,
And then began to eye his pipe,
    And then to pipe his eye.

And then he tried to sing 'All's Well',
    But could not though he tried;
His head was turned, and so he chewed
    His pigtail till he died.

His death, which happened in his berth
  At forty-odd befell:
They went and told the sexton, and
  The sexton tolled the bell.
THOMAS HOOD

Thomas Hood (1799–1845) was famous for his puns. A *blow* means hitting
somebody and also a strong wind. A *pressgang* was a group of men who
went round kidnapping young men for the Navy. *Boatswain* is usually
pronounced 'bo'sun'. *Eye-water* was used for eye complaints. *Benbow* was
a famous British admiral. A *tender* is a boat which goes between a large
ship and the shore. To *pipe his eye* means to shed tears. Sailors in those
days wore their hair in pigtails. A *berth* is the sleeping accommodation on
a ship.

JIM

Who ran away from his Nurse, and was eaten by a Lion.

There was a Boy whose name was Jim;
His Friends were very good to him.
They gave him Tea, and Cakes, and Jam,
And slices of delicious Ham,
And Chocolate with pink inside,
And little tricycles to ride,
And read him stories through and through,
And even took him to the Zoo—
But there it was the dreadful Fate
Befel him, which I now relate.

You know—at least you *ought* to know,
For I have often told you so—
That Children never are allowed
To leave their Nurses in a Crowd;
Now this was Jim's especial foible,
He ran away when he was able,
And on this inauspicious day
He slipped his hand and ran away!
He hadn't gone a yard when—
          Bang!
With open Jaws, a Lion sprang,
And hungrily began to eat
The Boy: beginning at his feet.

Now just imagine how it feels
When first your toes and then your heels,
And then by gradual degrees,
Your shins and ankles, calves and knees,
Are slowly eaten, bit by bit.
No wonder Jim detested it!
No wonder that he shouted 'Hi!'
The Honest Keeper heard his cry,
Though very fat, he almost ran
To help the little gentleman.

'Ponto!' he ordered as he came
(For Ponto was the Lion's name),
'Ponto!' he cried, with angry Frown.
'Let go, Sir! Down, Sir! Put it down!'

The Lion made a sudden stop,
He let the Dainty Morsel drop,
And slunk reluctant to his Cage,
Snarling with Disappointed Rage
But when he bent him over Jim,
The Honest Keeper's Eyes were dim.
The Lion having reached his Head,
The Miserable Boy was dead!

When Nurse informed his Parents, they
Were more Concerned than I can say:—
His Mqther, as She dried her eyes,
Said, 'Well—it gives me no surprise,
He would not do as he was told!'
His Father, who was self-controlled,
Bade all the children round attend
To James' miserable end,
And always keep a-hold of Nurse
For fear of finding something worse.

HILAIRE BELLOC

The Diverting History of John Gilpin

John Gilpin was a citizen
    Of credit and renown,
A train-band captain eke was he
    Of famous London town.

John Gilpin's spouse said to her dear:
    'Though wedded we have been
These twice ten tedious years, yet we
    No holiday have seen.

'To-morrow is our wedding-day,
    And we will then repair
Unto the Bell at Edmonton,
    All in a chaise and pair.

'My sister, and my sister's child,
    Myself, and children three,
Will fill the chaise; so you must ride
    On horseback after we.'

He soon replied: 'I do admire
    Of womankind but one,
And you are she, my dearest dear,
    Therefore it shall be done.

'I am a linen-draper bold,
    As all the world doth know,
And my good friend the calender
    Will lend his horse to go.'

Quoth Mrs. Gilpin: 'That's well said;
    And for that wine is dear,
We will be furnished with our own,
    Which is both bright and clear.'

John Gilpin kissed his loving wife;
    O'erjoyed was he to find,
That though on pleasure she was bent,
    She had a frugal mind.

The morning came, the chaise was brought,
    But yet was not allowed
To drive up to the door, lest all
    Should say that she was proud.

So three doors off the chaise was stayed,
    Where they did all get in;
Six precious souls, and all agog
    To dash through thick and thin.

Smack went the whip, round went the wheels,
    Were never folk so glad,
The stones did rattle underneath,
    As if Cheapside were mad.

John Gilpin at his horse's side
    Seized fast the flowing mane,
And up he got, in haste to ride,
    But soon came down again;

For saddle-tree scarce reached had he,
    His journey to begin,
When, turning round his head, he saw
    Three customers come in.

So down he came; for loss of time,
    Although it grieved him sore,
Yet loss of pence, full well he knew,
    Would trouble him much more.

'Twas long before the customers
    Were suited to their mind,
When Betty screaming came down stairs:
    'The wine is left behind!'

'Good lack!' quoth he, 'yet bring it me,
    My leathern belt likewise,
In which I bear my trusty sword,
    When I do exercise.'

Now Mistress Gilpin (careful soul!)
    Had two stone bottles found,
To hold the liquor that she loved,
    And keep it safe and sound.

Each bottle had a curling ear,
    Through which the belt he drew,
And hung a bottle on each side,
    To make his balance true.

Then over all, that he might be
    Equipped from top to toe,
His long red cloak, well brushed and neat,
    He manfully did throw.

Now see him mounted once again
    Upon his nimble steed,
Full slowly pacing o'er the stones,
    With caution and good heed.

But finding soon a smoother road
    Beneath his well-shod feet,
The snorting beast began to trot,
    Which galled him in his seat.

So, 'Fair and softly,' John he cried,
    But John he cried in vain;
That trot became a gallop soon,
    In spite of curb and rein.

So stooping down, as needs he must
    Who cannot sit upright,
He grasped the mane with both his hands,
    And eke with all his might.

His horse, who never in that sort
    Had handled been before,
What thing upon his back had got
    Did wonder more and more.

Away went Gilpin, neck or nought;
    Away went hat and wig;
He little dreamt, when he set out,
    Of running such a rig.

The wind did blow, the cloak did fly,
    Like streamer long and gay,
Till, loop and button failing both,
    At last it flew away.

Then might all people well discern
    The bottles he had slung;
A bottle swinging at each side,
    As hath been said or sung.

The dogs did bark, the children screamed,
    Up flew the windows all;
And every soul cried out: 'Well done!'
    As loud as he could bawl.

Away went Gilpin—who but he?
    His fame soon spread around;
'He carries weight!' 'He rides a race!'
    ''Tis for a thousand pound!'

And still, as fast as he drew near,
    'Twas wonderful to view,
How in a trice the turnpike-men
    Their gates wide open threw.

And now, as he went bowing down
    His reeking head full low,
The bottles twain behind his back
    Were shattered at a blow.

Down ran the wine into the road,
   Most piteous to be seen,
Which made his horse's flanks to smoke
   As they had basted been.

But still he seemed to carry weight,
   With leathern girdle braced;
For all might see the bottle-necks
   Still dangling at his waist.

Thus all through merry Islington
   These gambols he did play,
Until he came unto the Wash
   Of Edmonton so gay;

And there he threw the Wash about
   On both sides of the way,
Just like unto a trundling mop,
   Or a wild goose at play.

At Edmonton his loving wife
   From the balcony spied
Her tender husband, wondering much
   To see how he did ride.

'Stop, stop, John Gilpin! Here's the house!'
   They all at once did cry;
'The dinner waits, and we are tired.'
   Said Gilpin: 'So am I!'

But yet his horse was not a whit
   Inclined to tarry there!
For why?—his owner had a house
   Full ten miles off, at Ware.

So like an arrow swift he flew,
   Shot by an archer strong;
So did he fly—which brings me to
   The middle of my song.

Away went Gilpin, out of breath,
    And sore against his will,
Till at his friend the calender's
    His horse at last stood still.

The calender, amazed to see
    His neighbour in such trim,
Laid down his pipe, flew to the gate,
    And thus accosted him:

'What news? what news? your tidings tell;
    Tell me you must and shall—
Say why bareheaded you are come,
    Or why you come at all?'

Now Gilpin had a pleasant wit,
    And loved a timely joke;
And thus unto the calender
    In merry guise he spoke:

'I came because your horse would come,
    And, if I well forebode,
My hat and wig will soon be here;
    They are upon the road.'

The calender, right glad to find
    His friend in merry pin,
Returned him not a single word,
    But to the house went in;

Whence straight he came with hat and wig;
    A wig that flowed behind,
A hat not much the worse for wear,
    Each comely in its kind.

He held them up, and in his turn
    Thus showed his ready wit,
'My head is twice as big as yours,
    They therefore needs must fit.

'But let me scrape the dirt away
    That hangs upon your face;
And stop and eat, for well you may
    Be in a hungry case.'

Said John: 'It is my wedding-day,
    And all the world would stare,
If wife should dine at Edmonton,
    And I should dine at Ware.'

So, turning to his horse, he said,
    'I am in haste to dine;
'Twas for your pleasure you came here,
    You shall go back for mine.'

Ah, luckless speech, and bootless boast!
    For which he paid full dear;
For, while he spake, a braying ass
    Did sing most loud and clear;

Whereat his horse did snort, as he
    Had heard a lion roar,
And galloped off with all his might,
    As he had done before.

Away went Gilpin, and away
    Went Gilpin's hat and wig:
He lost them sooner than at first;
    For why?—they were too big.

Now Mistress Gilpin, when she saw
    Her husband posting down
Into the country far away,
    She pulled out half a crown;

And thus unto the youth she said
    That drove them to the Bell,
'This shall be yours, when you bring back
    My husband safe and well.'

The youth did ride, and soon did meet
    John coming back amain,
Whom in a trice he tried to stop
    By catching at his rein;

But not performing what he meant,
    And gladly would have done,
The frighted steed he frighted more,
    And made him faster run.

Away went Gilpin, and away
    Went postboy at his heels,
The postboy's horse right glad to miss
    The lumbering of the wheels.

Six gentlemen upon the road,
    Thus seeing Gilpin fly,
With postboy scampering in the rear,
    They raised the hue and cry:

'Stop thief! stop thief!—a highwayman!'
   Not one of them was mute;
And all and each that passed that way
   Did join in the pursuit.

And now the turnpike gates again
   Flew open in short space;
The toll-men thinking, as before,
   That Gilpin rode a race.

And so he did, and won it too,
   For he got first to town;
Nor stopped till where he had got up
   He did again get down.

Now let us sing: Long live the king!
   And Gilpin, long live he!
And when he next doth ride abroad
   May I be there to see!

WILLIAM COWPER

This poem is a comic imitation of the old ballads. *Eke*, for example, is a
very old word for 'too'. A *train-band captain* is much the same as an officer
in the Territorial Army to-day. A *citizen* is someone who lives in the City
of London and lives by trade. A *chaise* is a kind of carriage. A *calender* is a
man who prepares cloth by pressing it. *Betty* is the servant. '*He carries
weight*' means that he had weights on him as a handicap (this is still done
in horse-racing). *Turnpikes* were the gates where travellers had to pay
before they were allowed through; this money paid for the upkeep of the
roads. *Basting* is pouring fat or wine over something that is being roasted.
On the road means 'on the way' as well as 'lying in the road' (this is
Gilpin's joke). *Half a crown* ($12\frac{1}{2}$p) would, in those days, have been worth
a pound or two.

The Yarn of the 'Nancy Bell'

'Twas on the shores that round our coast
 From Deal to Ramsgate span,
That I found alone on a piece of stone
 An elderly naval man.

His hair was weedy, his beard was long,
 And weedy and long was he,
And I heard this wight on the shore recite,
 In a singular minor key:

'Oh, I am a cook and a captain bold,
 And the mate of the *Nancy* brig,
And a bo'sun tight, and a midshipmite,
 And the crew of the captain's gig.'

And he shook his fists and he tore his hair,
 Till I really felt afraid.
For I couldn't help thinking the man had been drinking,
 And so I simply said:

'Oh, elderly man, it's little I know
 Of the duties of men of the sea,
And I'll eat my hand if I understand
 How you can possibly be

At once a cook, and a captain bold,
 And the mate of the *Nancy* brig,
And a bo'sun tight and a midshipmite,
 And the crew of the captain's gig.'

Then he gave a hitch to his trousers, which
 Is a trick all seamen larn,
And having got rid of a thumping quid,
 He spun this painful yarn:

''Twas in the good ship, *Nancy Bell*,
 That we sailed to the Indian Sea,
And there on a reef we come to grief,
 Which has often occurred to me.

And pretty nigh all o' the crew was drowned
    (There was seventy-seven o' soul)
And only ten of the *Nancy's* men
    Said 'Here!' to the muster roll.

There was me and the cook and the captain bold,
    And the mate of the *Nancy* brig,
And the bo'sun tight and a midshipmite,
    And the crew of the captain's gig.

For a month we'd neither wittles nor drink,
    Till a-hungry we did feel,
So we drawed a lot, and accordin' shot
    The captain for our meal.

The next lot fell to the *Nancy's* mate,
    And a delicate dish he made;
Then our appetite with the midshipmite
    We seven survivors stayed.

And then we murdered the bo'sun tight,
    And he much resembled pig;
Then we wittled free, did the cook and me,
    On the crew of the captain's gig.

Then only the cook and me was left,
    And the delicate question, 'Which
Of us two go to the kettle?'' arose,
    And we argued it out as sich.

For I loved that cook as a brother, I did,
    And the cook he worshipped me;
But we'd both be blowed if we'd either be stowed
    In the other chap's hold, you see.

"I'll be eat if you dines off me," says Tom,
    "Yes, that," says I, "you'll be"—
"I'm boiled if I die, my friend," quoth I,
    And "exactly so," quoth he.

Says he, "Dear James, to murder me
 Were a foolish thing to do,
For don't you see that you can't cook *me*,
 While I can—and will—cook *you*!"

So he boils the water, and takes the salt
 And the pepper in portions true
(Which he never forgot) and some chopped shalot
 And some sage and parsley too.

"Come here," says he, with a proper pride,
 Which his smiling features tell,
"'Twill soothing be if I let you see,
 How extremely nice you'll smell."

And he stirred it round and round and round,
 And he sniffed at the foaming froth;
When I ups his heels, and smothers his squeals
 In the scum of the boiling broth.

And I eat that cook in a week or less,
 And—as I eating be
The last of his chops, why I almost drops,
 For a vessel in sight I see.

*　　*　　*

And I never grieve, and I never smile,
 And I never larf nor play,
But I sit and croak, and a single joke
 I have—which is to say:

Oh, I am a cook and a captain bold,
 And the mate of the *Nancy* brig,
And a bo'sun tight, and a midshipmite,
 And the crew of the captain's gig!'

W. S. GILBERT

Larn is 'learn'. *Got rid of a thumping quid* means that he spat out a large
lump of tobacco. Chewing tobacco was very popular at one time.

George II and the Chinese Emperor

Prince George of Hanover was thirty-one
When first he came to London (as the son
Of George I) but came resolved to stay,
Though speaking English in a German way,
And when his father died was duly reckoned
Heir to the Throne; so reigned as George the Second.
All England thought more highly of him when
He put the French to rout at Dettingen.
(Alas, he lost his saddle, reins and horse,
But kept his royal dignity—of course.)

One fine day, news arrived from the Far East
That made George somewhat cross, to say the least.
He called in loud tones, which I hardly think
We should dare imitate: 'Fetch pen and ink.
I'll write a threatening note in my own hand.
This Chinese Emperor must understand
We English have good reason when we brag:
No heathen shall insult our glorious flag.
Two Bristol ships at Hankow fetching tea,
Boarded and robbed in harbour as they lay,
Of a costly cargo! Ha, Sir, let me boast
Our fleet stands ready to bombard your coast.
If meek apologies be not forthcoming
My Fusiliers will through Pekin go drumming.
You must eat dirt, d'ye hear, you knavish fellow,
Or we shall tan your hide a deeper yellow.
Ten ships a year will visit your chief ports
With mirrors, beads, and cottons of all sorts,
Carrying nobly to your savage parts
Some slight veneer of culture and the arts;
But if so much as a tea-pot's robbed or broke,
Your Chinese territory flies up in smoke.
Beware, you rogue! Signed GEORGIUS REX. So, so.
Our Foreign Minister sends this. Take it, go!'

The Foreign Minister, reading the Note through,
Swore by his wig, why, this would never do.
'Our Sovereign trips on all the finer points
Of the King's English: muddles and disjoints.
To send this letter would be far from wise—
Suppose that it were captured by French spies!
Why, even a Chinaman might laugh to read
This blotted, badly penned, Teutonic screed.
But stay! Our Sovereign we should surely please
If we translated it into Chinese . . .
Li Chung can do't, and there will be no call
To keep a record of the original.'

Li Chung, a Bond Street tea-man with meek eyes,
Performed the service, showing no surprise,
Though inwardly enraged and jealous for
The honour of his Godlike Emperor . . .
How faithful his translation, who can say?
George signed and sealed and sent it to Cathay.

The famed Kien Lung, now ruling at Pekin
(But Tartar, not Chinese, by origin),
Read Li-Chung's Note, set down his fragrant drink,
Shouted for sable paint-brushes and ink,
And, in his own hand, wrote a Dispensation,
'*To the Loyal Governor of the British Nation*:
While sympathizing with that luckless one,
By seas exiled from our Imperial Sun,
For his outcast and woe-begone condition,
We note the servile tone of this petition,
And long excuses for his impudence
In thus disturbing our Magnificence.
So, though we cannot in the Atlas hit on
A Chinese province (or sub-province) *Britain*,
We graciously will, none the less, allow
Ten junks a year to anchor at Hankow
With oil, logs, skins, and other paltry stuff—
Indeed, five junk-loads would be quite enough.
Signed, GODLIKE EMPEROR, KIEN LUNG. So, so.
Our Frontier Minister sends this. Take it, go!'

The Frontier Minister, reading the piece through,
Swore by his pigtail: 'This will never do!
Why, every line neglects the niceties,
Indeed, the simpler rules, of Court Chinese.
Our Tartar Warrior-god, in battle's shock
Or council-chamber, sits as firm as rock,
But as for penning an Imperial letter,
My youngest child could do as well, nay, better!
Can I permit my Sovereign's reputation
To sink even in a heathen's estimation?
I'll tell him tactfully, 'tis more correct
To send the Note in British dialect.
Ned Gunn, the boxing-teacher at Chang-Ching
Will soon translate it for his abject King.'

Ned Gunn, a stolid sailor with bold eyes,
Performed the service, showing no surprise
Though, loyal to the death, he felt his gorge
Rise at this insult to victorious George . . .
The Emperor signed, sealed and sent off by sea
Ned Gunn's translation—which was somewhat free.

George read the Note, puffed out his chest, began
Chuckling and said: 'This funny Chinaman
Apologizes humbly, swears to behave
As loyally as lap-dog or as slave,
Admits his colour's far from honest white
But trusts his language is not impolite;
Longs for our British cargoes rich and strange;
Has only trash to offer in exchange—
"May your Red, White and Blue still rule the main
And countless Dettingens be fought again!
God Save the King! Kow Tow! Success to Barter!"'

George swore: 'I shall reward him with the Garter.'

ROBERT GRAVES

The Dong with a Luminous Nose

When awful darkness and silence reign
Over the great Gromboolian plain,
   Through the long, long wintry nights;—
When the angry breakers roar
As they beat on the rocky shore;—
   When Storm-clouds brood on the towering heights
Of the Hills of the Chankly Bore:—

Then, through the vast and gloomy dark,
There moves what seems a fiery spark,
   A lonely spark with silvery rays
   Piercing the coal-black night,—
   A meteor strange and bright:—
Hither and thither the vision strays,
   A single lurid light.

Slowly it wanders,—pauses,—creeps,—
Anon it sparkles,—flashes and leaps;
And ever as onward it gleaming goes
A light on the Bong-tree stems it throws.
And those who watch at that midnight hour
From Hall or Terrace, or lofty Tower,
Cry, as the wild light passes along,—
     'The Dong!—the Dong!
    'The wandering Dong through the forest goes!
     'The Dong! the Dong!
    'The Dong with a luminous Nose!'

     Long years ago
   The Dong was happy and gay,
Till he fell in love with a Jumbly Girl
   Who came to those shores one day.
For the Jumblies came in a Sieve, they did,—
Landing at eve near the Zemmery Fidd
    Where the Oblong Oysters grow,
   And the rocks are smooth and gray.

And all the woods and the valleys rang
With the Chorus they daily and nightly sang,—
  'Far and few, far and few,
  Are the lands where the Jumblies live;
  Their heads are green, and their hands are blue,
  And they went to sea in a Sieve."

Happily, happily passed those days!
  While the cheerful Jumblies staid;
  They danced in circlets all night long,
  To the plaintive pipe of the lively Dong,
    In moonlight, shine, or shade.
For day and night he was always there
By the side of the Jumbly Girl so fair,
With her sky-blue hands, and her sea-green hair,
Till the morning came of that hateful day
When the Jumblies sailed in their Sieve away,

And the Dong was left on the cruel shore
Gazing—gazing for evermore,—
Ever keeping his weary eyes on
That pea-green sail on the far horizon,—
Singing the Jumbly Chorus still
As he sate all day on the grassy hill,—
  'Far and few, far and few,
  Are the lands where the Jumblies live;
  Their heads are green, and their hands are blue,
  And they went to sea in a Sieve."

But when the sun was low in the West,
  The Dong arose and said,—
  'What little sense I once possessed
  'Has quite gone out of my head!'
And since that day he wanders still
By lake and forest, marsh and hill,
Singing—'O somewhere, in valley or plain
'Might I find my Jumbly Girl again!
'For ever I'll seek by lake and shore
'Till I find my Jumbly Girl once more!'

47

Playing a pipe with silvery squeaks,
Since then his Jumbly Girl he seeks,
And because by night he could not see,
He gathered the bark of the Twangum Tree
    On the flowery plain that grows.
    And he wove him a wondrous Nose,—
A Nose as strange as a Nose could be!
Of vast proportions and painted red,
And tied with cords to the back of his head.
    —In a hollow rounded space it ended
    With a luminous lamp within suspended
        All fenced about
        With a bandage stout
        To prevent the wind from blowing it out;—
And with holes all round to send the light,
In gleaming rays on the dismal night.

And now each night, and all night long,
Over those plains still roams the Dong;
And above the wail of the Chimp and Snipe
You may hear the squeak of his plaintive pipe
While ever he seeks, but seeks in vain
To meet with his Jumbly Girl again;
Lonely and wild—all night he goes,—
The Dong with a luminous Nose!
And all who watch at the midnight hour,
From Hall or Terrace, or lofty Tower,
Cry, as they trace the Meteor bright,
Moving along through the dreary night,—
    'This is the hour when forth he goes,
    'The Dong with a luminous Nose!
    'Yonder—over the plain he goes;
        'He goes!
        'He goes;
    'The Dong with a luminous Nose!'

EDWARD LEAR

Little Billee

There were three sailors of Bristol City
   Who took a boat and went to sea,
But first with beef and captain's biscuits,
   And pickled pork they loaded she.

There was gorging Jack, and guzzling Jimmy,
   And the youngest he was little Billee.
Now when they'd got as far as the Equator,
   They'd nothing left but one split pea.

Says gorging Jack to guzzling Jimmy,
   'I am extremely hungaree.'
To gorging Jack says guzzling Jimmy,
   'We've nothing left, us must eat we.'

Says gorging Jack to guzzling Jimmy,
   'With one another we shouldn't agree!
There's little Bill, he's young and tender,
   We're old and tough, so let's eat he.'

'O Billy! we're going to kill and eat you,
    So undo the button of your chemie.'
When Bill received this information,
    He used his pocket handkerchie.

'First let me say my catechism,
    Which my poor mother taught to me.'
'Make haste! make haste!' says guzzling Jimmy,
    While Jack pulled out his snicker-snee.

Then Bill went up to the main-top-gallant-mast,
    And down he fell on his bended knee,
He scarce had come to the Twelfth Commandment
    When up he jumps—'There's land I see!'

'Jerusalem and Madagascar,
    And North and South Amerikee,
There's the British flag a-riding at anchor,
    With Admiral Napier, K.C.B.'

So when they got aboard of the Admiral's,
    He hanged fat Jack and flogged Jimmee,
But as for little Bill, he made him
    The captain of a Seventy-three.

W. M. THACKERAY

Chemie is chemise, a kind of vest. A *snicker-snee* is a knife. A *Seventy-three* is a sailing ship with 73 guns.

Epicurean Reminiscences of a Sentimentalist

'My *Tables*! *Meat* it is, *I set it* down!'—*Hamlet*

I think it was Spring—but not certain I am—
    When my passion began first to work;
But I know we were certainly looking for lamb,
    And the season was over for pork.

'Twas at Christmas, I think, when I met with Miss Chase,
    Yes,—for Morris had asked me to dine,—
And I thought I had never beheld such a face,
    Or so noble a turkey and chine.

Placed close to her side, it made others quite wild,
    With sheer envy to witness my luck;
How she blushed as I gave her some turtle, and smiled
    As I afterwards offered some duck.

I looked and I languished, alas, to my cost,
    Through three courses of dishes and meats;
Getting deeper in love—but my heart was quite lost,
    When it came to the trifle and sweets!

With a rent-roll that told of my houses and land
    To her parents I told my designs—
And then to herself I presented my hand,
    With a very fine pottle of pines!

I asked her to have me for weal or for woe,
    And she did not object in the least:
I can't tell the date—but we married, I know,
    Just in time to have game at the feast.

We went to ——, it certainly was the seaside;
    For the next, the most blessed of morns,
I remember how fondly I gazed at my bride,
    Sitting down to a plateful of prawns.

Oh, never may mem'ry lose sight of that year,
    But still hallow the time as it ought,
That season the 'grass' was remarkably dear,
    And the peas at a guinea a quart.

So happy, like hours, all our days seemed to haste,
    A fond pair, such as poets have drawn,
So united in heart—so congenial in taste,
    We were both of us partial to brawn!

A long life I looked for of bliss with my bride,
    But then Death—I ne'er dreamt about that!
Oh, there's nothing certain in life, as I cried,
    When my turbot eloped with the cat!

My dearest took ill at the turn of the year,
　But the cause no physician could nab;
But something it seemed like consumption, I fear,
　It was just after supping on crab.

In vain she was doctored, in vain she was dosed,
　Still her strength and her appetite pined;
She lost relish for what she had relished the most,
　Even salmon she deeply declined.

For months still I lingered in hope and in doubt,
　While her form it grew wasted and thin;
But the last dying spark of existence went out,
　As the oysters were just coming in!

She died, and she left me the saddest of men
　To indulge in a widower's moan;
Oh, I felt all the power of solitude then,
　As I ate my first natives alone!

But when I beheld Virtue's friends in their cloaks,
　And with sorrowful crape on their hats,
Oh, my grief poured a flood! and the out-of-door folks
　Were all crying—I think it was sprats!

THOMAS HOOD

This is a poem about a very greedy man. The *Epicureans* were the
followers of the Ancient Greek philosopher Epicurus, who taught that
people should enjoy themselves while they could.
A *chine* of beef is a piece of meat. *Turtle* is turtle soup. A *pottle* is a wicker
basket. *Pines* are pineapples. *Game* is the meat of deer, pheasant, grouse,
rabbit, hare, etc. '*Grass*' is asparagus. *Turbot* is a large flat fish.
Consumption is tuberculosis (a disease of the lungs) but also means eating.
Natives are 'native' oysters. '*Crying sprats*' would be one of the 'cries' of
the street-sellers.

The Droll Tale of the Old Woman Who Bought a Pig

An old woman went to market and bought a pig;
Pig had four legs,
But pig would not go.
Well, says the old woman, what shall I do?

She went a little farther and she calls to a dog,
Dog, dog, bite pig,
Pig will not go,
And I should have been at home two hours ago.
   But the dog would not.

She went a little farther and she calls to a stick,
Stick, stick, beat dog,
Dog won't bite pig,
Pig will not go,
And I should have been at home two hours ago.
   But the stick would not.

She went a little farther and she calls to a fire,
Fire, fire, burn stick,
Stick won't beat dog,
Dog won't bite pig,
Pig will not go,
And I should have been at home two hours ago.
   But the fire would not.

She went a little farther and she calls to some water,
Water, water, quench fire,
Fire won't burn stick,
Stick won't beat dog,
Dog won't bite pig,
Pig will not go,
And I should have been at home two hours ago.
   But the water would not.

She went a little farther and she calls to an ox,
Ox, ox, drink water,
Water won't quench fire,
Fire won't burn stick,
Stick won't beat dog,
Dog won't bite pig,
Pig will not go,
And I should have been at home two hours ago.
    But the ox would not.

She went a little farther and she calls to a butcher,
Butcher, butcher, kill ox,
Ox won't drink water,
Water won't quench fire,
Fire won't burn stick,
Stick won't beat dog,
Dog won't bite pig,
Pig will not go,
And I should have been at home two hours ago.
    But the butcher would not.

She went a little farther and she calls to a rope,
Rope, rope, hang butcher,
Butcher won't kill ox,
Ox won't drink water,
Water won't quench fire,
Fire won't burn stick,
Stick won't beat dog,
Dog won't bite pig,
Pig will not go,
And I should have been at home two hours ago.
    But the rope would not.

She went a little farther and she calls to a rat,
Rat, rat, gnaw rope,
Rope won't hang butcher,
Butcher won't kill ox,
Ox won't drink water,
Water won't quench fire,
Fire won't burn stick,
Stick won't beat dog,

Dog won't bite pig,
Pig will not go,
And I should have been at home two hours ago.
  But the rat would not.

She went a little farther and she calls to a cat,
Cat, cat, kill rat,
Rat won't gnaw rope,
Rope won't hang butcher,
Butcher won't kill ox,
Ox won't drink water,
Water won't quench fire,
Fire won't burn stick,
Stick won't beat dog,
Dog won't bite pig,
Pig will not go,
And I should have been at home two hours ago.

Then the cat began to kill the rat,
The rat began to gnaw the rope,
The rope began to hang the butcher,
The butcher began to kill the ox,
The ox began to drink the water,
The water began to quench the fire,
The fire began to burn the stick,
The stick began to beat the dog,
The dog began to bite the pig,
The pig began to go;
  So it's all over, and the old woman's home again now.

ANONYMOUS

The Three Little Kittens

Three little kittens
They lost their mittens,
  And they began to cry,
Oh, mother dear,
We sadly fear
  Our mittens we have lost.
What! lost your mittens,
You naughty kittens!
  Then you shall have no pie.
  Mee-ow, mee-ow, mee-ow.
  No, you shall have no pie.

The three little kittens
They found their mittens,
  And they began to cry,
Oh, mother dear,
See here, see here,
  Our mittens we have found.
Put on your mittens,
You silly kittens,
  And you shall have some pie.
  Purr-r, purr-r, purr-r,
  Oh, let us have some pie.

The three little kittens
Put on their mittens
  And soon ate up the pie;
Oh, mother dear,
We greatly fear
  Our mittens we have soiled.
What! soiled your mittens,
You naughty kittens!
  Then they began to sigh,
  Mee-ow, mee-ow, mee-ow,
  Then they began to sigh.

The three little kittens
They washed their mittens,
   And hung them out to dry;
Oh! mother dear,
Do you not hear,
   Our mittens we have washed.
What! washed your mittens,
Then you're good kittens,
   But I smell a rat close by.
   Mee-ow, mee-ow, mee-ow,
   We smell a rat close by.

ANONYMOUS

Sir Walter Raleigh Sailing in the Low-lands

Sir Walter Raleigh has built a Ship
                in the Neatherlands,
Sir Walter Raleigh has built a Ship
                in the Neatherlands,
And it is called the sweet Trinity,
And was taken by the false Gallaly,
                sailing in the Low-lands.

Is there never a seaman bold
                in the Neatherlands?
Is there never a seaman bold
                in the Neatherlands?
That will go take this false Gallaly,
And to redeem the sweet Trinity,
                sailing in the Low-lands.

Then spoke the little Ship boy
   in the Neatherlands,
Then spoke the little Ship boy
   in the Neatherlands,
Master, Master, what will you give me?
And I will take this false Gallaly,
And release the sweet Trinity,
   sailing in the Low-lands.

I'll give thee gold, and I'll give thee fee,
   in the Neatherlands,
I'll give thee gold, and I'll give thee fee,
   in the Neatherlands,
And my eldest daughter thy wife shall be,
   sailing in the Low-lands.

He had an augur fit for the nonce,
   in the Neatherlands,
He had an augur fit for the nonce,
   in the Neatherlands,
The which will bore fifteen good holes at once,
   sailing in the Low-lands.

Some were at cards, and some at dice,
   in the Neatherlands,
Some were at cards, and some at dice,
   in the Neatherlands,
Until the salt water flashed in their eyes,
   sailing in the Low-lands.

Some cut their hats and some their caps,
   in the Neatherlands,
Some cut their hats and some their caps,
   in the Neatherlands,
For to stop the salt-water gaps,
   sailing in the Low-lands.

He set his breast and away did swim,
   in the Neatherlands,
He set his breast and away did swim,
   in the Neatherlands,

Until he came to his own Ship again,
                    sailing in the Low-lands.

I have done the work I have promised to do,
                    in the Neatherlands,
I have done the work I have promised to do,
                    in the Neatherlands,
For I have sunk the false Gallaly,
And released the sweet Trinity,
                    sailing in the Low-lands.

You promised me gold, and you promised me fee,
                    in the Neatherlands.
You promised me gold and you promised me fee,
                    in the Neatherlands.
Your eldest daughter my Wife she must be,
                    sailing in the Low-lands.

You shall have gold, and you shall have fee,
                    in the Neatherlands,
You shall have gold, and you shall have fee,
                    in the Neatherlands,
But my eldest daughter your Wife shall never be,
                    sailing in the Low-lands.

Then fare you well, you cozening Lord,
                    in the Neatherlands.
Then fare you well, you cozening Lord,
                    in the Neatherlands.
Seeing you are not as good as your word,
                    for sailing in the Low-lands.

And thus I shall conclude my Song,
                    of the sailing in the Low-lands,
And thus I shall conclude my Song,
                    of the sailing in the Low-lands.
Wishing happiness to all Seamen, old or young,
                    in their sailing in the Low-lands.

ANONYMOUS

An *augur* is a drill.

62

The Jumblies

I

They went to sea in a Sieve, they did,
   In a Sieve they went to sea:
In spite of all their friends could say,
On a winter's morn, on a stormy day,
   In a Sieve they went to sea!
And when the Sieve turned round and round,
And every one cried, 'You'll all be drowned!'
They called aloud, 'Our Sieve ain't big,
'But we don't care a button! we don't care a fig!
   'In a Sieve we'll go to sea!'
   Far and few, far and few,
      Are the lands where the Jumblies live;
      Their heads are green, and their hands are blue,
      And they went to sea in a Sieve.

II

They sailed away in a Sieve, they did,
   In a Sieve they sailed so fast,
With only a beautiful pea-green veil
Tied with a riband by way of a sail,
   To a small tobacco-pipe mast;
And every one said, who saw them go,
'O won't they be soon upset, you know!
'For the sky is dark, and the voyage is long,
'And happen what may, it's extremely wrong
   'In a Sieve to sail so fast!'
   Far and few, far and few,
      Are the lands where the Jumblies live;
      Their heads are green, and their hands are blue,
      And they went to sea in a Sieve.

III

The water it soon came in, it did,
   The water it soon came in;
So to keep them dry, they wrapped their feet
In a pinky paper all folded neat,
   And they fastened it down with a pin.

And they passed the night in a crockery-jar,
And each of them said, 'How wise we are!
'Though the sky be dark, and the voyage be long,
'Yet we never can think we were rash or wrong,
  'While round in our Sieve we spin!'
  Far and few, far and few,
      Are the lands where the Jumblies live;
  Their heads are green, and their hands are blue,
      And they went to sea in a Sieve.

                    IV
And all night long they sailed away;
    And when the sun went down,
They whistled and warbled a moony song
To the echoing sound of a coppery gong,
    In the shade of the mountains brown.
'O Timballo! How happy we are,
'When we live in a sieve and a crockery-jar.
'And all night long in the moonlight pale,
'We sail away with a pea-green sail,
    'In the shade of the mountains brown!'
  Far and few, far and few,
      Are the lands where the Jumblies live;
  Their heads are green, and their hands are blue,
      And they went to sea in a Sieve.

                    V
They sailed to the Western Sea, they did,
    To a land all covered with trees,
And they bought an Owl, and a useful Cart,
And a pound of Rice, and a Cranberry Tart,
    And a hive of silvery Bees.
And they bought a Pig, and some green Jackdaws,
And a lovely Monkey with lollipop paws,
And forty bottles of Ring-Bo-Ree,
    And no end of Stilton Cheese.
  Far and few, far and few,
      Are the lands where the Jumblies live;
  Their heads are green, and their hands are blue,
      And they went to sea in a Sieve.

VI

And in twenty years they all came back,
    In twenty years or more,
And every one said, 'How tall they've grown!
'For they've been to the Lakes, and the Terrible Zone,
    'And the hills of the Chankly Bore;'
And they drank their health, and gave them a feast
Of dumplings made of beautiful yeast;
And every one said, 'If we only live,
'We too will go to sea in a Sieve,—
    'To the hills of the Chankly Bore!'
    Far and few, far and few,
        Are the lands where the Jumblies live;
    Their heads are green, and their hands are blue,
        And they went to sea in a Sieve.

EDWARD LEAR

2. SONGS AND SO ON

The Twelve Days of Christmas

The first day of Christmas
My true love sent to me
A partridge in a pear tree.

The second day of Christmas
My true love sent to me
Two turtle doves, and
A partridge in a pear tree.

The third day of Christmas
My true love sent to me
Three French hens,
Two turtle doves, and
A partridge in a pear tree.

The fourth day of Christmas
My true love sent to me
Four colly birds,
Three French hens,
Two turtle doves, and
A partridge in a pear tree.

The fifth day of Christmas
My true love sent to me
Five gold rings,
Four colly birds,
Three French hens,
Two turtle doves, and
A partridge in a pear tree.

The sixth day of Christmas
My true love sent to me
Six geese a-laying,
Five gold rings,
Four colly birds,
Three French hens,
Two turtle doves, and
A partridge in a pear tree.

The seventh day of Christmas
My true love sent to me
Seven swans a-swimming,
Six geese a-laying,
Five gold rings,
Four colly birds,
Three French hens,
Two turtle doves, and
A partridge in a pear tree.

The eighth day of Christmas
My true love sent to me
Eight maids a-milking,
Seven swans a-swimming,
Six geese a-laying,
Five gold rings,
Four colly birds,
Three French hens,
Two turtle doves, and
A partridge in a pear tree.

The ninth day of Christmas
My true love sent to me
Nine drummers drumming,
Eight maids a-milking,
Seven swans a-swimming,
Six geese a-laying,
Five gold rings,
Four colly birds,
Three French hens,
Two turtle doves, and
A partridge in a pear tree.

The tenth day of Christmas
My true love sent to me
Ten pipers piping,
Nine drummers drumming,
Eight maids a-milking,
Seven swans a-swimming,
Six geese a-laying,
Five gold rings,

Four colly birds,
Three French hens,
Two turtle doves, and
A partridge in a pear tree.

The eleventh day of Christmas
My true love sent to me
Eleven ladies dancing,
Ten pipers piping,
Nine drummers drumming,
Eight maids a-milking,
Seven swans a-swimming,
Six geese a-laying,
Five gold rings,
Four colly birds,
Three French hens,
Two turtle doves, and
A partridge in a pear tree.

The twelfth day of Christmas
My true love sent to me
Twelve lords a-leaping,
Eleven ladies dancing,
Ten pipers piping,
Nine drummers drumming,
Eight maids a-milking,
Seven swans a-swimming,
Six geese a-laying,
Five gold rings,
Four colly birds,
Three French hens,
Two turtle doves, and
A partridge in a pear tree.

ANONYMOUS

Lines from The Gardener's Song in 'Sylvie and Bruno'

He thought he saw a Banker's clerk
    Descending from the 'bus;
He looked again, and found it was
    A Hippopotamus.
'If this should stay to dine,' he said,
    'There won't be much for us!'

He thought he saw an Albatross
    That fluttered round the lamp:
He looked again, and found it was
    A Penny-Postage-Stamp.
'You'd best be getting home,' he said;
    'The nights are very damp!'

He thought he saw a Coach-and-Four
    That stood beside his bed:
He looked again, and found it was
    A Bear without a Head.
'Poor thing,' he said, 'poor silly thing!
    It's waiting to be fed!'

He thought he saw a Kangaroo
    That worked a coffee-mill:
He looked again, and found it was
    A Vegetable-Pill.
'Were I to swallow this,' he said,
    'I should be very ill!'

He thought he saw a Rattlesnake
    That questioned him in Greek:
He looked again, and found it was
    The Middle of Next Week.
'The one thing I regret,' he said,
    'Is that it cannot speak!'

LEWIS CARROLL

Elves' Song

Buz! quoth the blue fly;
 Hum! quoth the bee:
Buz! and Hum! they cry,
 And so do we.
In his ear, in his nose,
 Thus do you see?
He ate the dormouse:
 Else it was he.

BEN JONSON

Bagpipes

Puss came dancing out of a barn
With a pair of bagpipes under her arm;
She could sing nothing but, Fiddle cum fee,
The mouse has married the humble-bee.
Pipe, cat—dance, mouse—
We'll have a wedding at our good house.

ANONYMOUS

Tongue-Twister

Theophilus Thistledown, the successful thistle sifter,
In sifting a sieve of unsifted thistles,
Thrust three thousand thistles
Through the thick of his thumb.
If, then, Theophilus Thistledown, the successful thistle
   sifter,
In sifting a sieve full of unsifted thistles,
Thrust three thousand thistles
Through the thick of his thumb,
See that thou, in sifting a sieve of unsifted thistles,
Do not get the unsifted thistles stuck in thy tongue.

ANONYMOUS

Boys and Girls Come Out to Play

Boys and girls come out to play,
The moon doth shine as bright as day.
Leave your supper and leave your sleep,
And join your playfellows in the street.
Come with a whoop and come with a call,
Come with a good will or not at all.
Up the ladder and down the wall,
A half-penny loaf will serve us all;
You find milk, and I'll find flour,
And we'll have a pudding in half an hour.

ANONYMOUS

The Constant Lover

Though regions far divided
    And tedious tracts of time,
By my misfortune guided,
    Make absence thought a crime;
Though we were set asunder
    As far, as East from West,
Love still would work this wonder,
    Thou shouldst be in my breast.

How slow, alas, are paces,
    Compared to thoughts that fly
In moment back to places
    Whole ages scarce descry.
The body must have pauses;
    The mind requires no rest;
Love needs no second causes
    To guide thee to my breast.

Accept in that poor dwelling
    But welcome, nothing great,
With pride no turrets swelling,
    But lowly as the seat
Where, though not much delighted,
    In peace thou mayst be blest,
Unfeasted yet unfrighted
    By rivals, in my breast.

But this is not the diet
    That doth for glory strive;
Poor beauties seek in quiet
    To keep one heart alive,
The price of his ambition,
    That looks for such a guest,
Is hopeless of fruition,
    To beat an empty breast.

See then my last lamenting:
    Upon a cliff I'll sit,
Rock Constancy presenting,
    Till I grow part of it;
My tears a quicksand feeding,
    Whereon no foot can rest,
My sighs a tempest breeding
    About my stony breast.

Those arms, wherein wide open
    Love's fleet was wont to put,
Shall laid across betoken
    That haven's mouth is shut.
Mine eyes no light shall cherish
    For ships at sea distressed,
But darkling let them perish
    Or split against my breast.

Yet if I can discover
    When thine before it rides,
To show I was thy lover
    I'll smooth my rugged sides;
And so much better measure
    Afford thee than the rest,
Thou shalt have no displeasure
    By knocking at my breast.

AURELIAN TOWNSEND

Jingle

Hoddley, poddley, puddle and fogs,
Cats are to marry the poodle dogs;
Cats in blue jackets and dogs in red hats,
What will become of the mice and the rats?

ANONYMOUS

Five Toes

The pettitoes are little feet,
  And the little feet not big;
Great feet belong to the grunting hog,
  And the pettitoes to the little pig.

ANONYMOUS

Calico Pie

I

Calico Pie,
The little Birds fly
Down to the calico tree,
　Their wings were blue,
　And they sang 'Tilly-loo!'
　Till away they flew,—
And they never came back to me!
　They never came back!
　They never came back!
They never came back to me!

II

Calico Jam,
The little Fish swam
Over the syllabub sea,
　He took off his hat,
　To the Sole and the Sprat,
　And the Willeby-wat,—
But he never came back to me!
　He never came back!
　He never came back!
He never came back to me!

III

Calico Ban,
The little Mice ran,
To be ready in time for tea,
　Flippity flup,
　They drank it all up,
　And danced in the cup,—
But they never came back to me!
　They never came back!
　They never came back!
They never came back to me!

IV
Calico Drum,
  The Grasshoppers come,
The Butterfly, Beetle, and Bee,
  Over the ground,
  Around and round,
  With a hop and a bound,—
But they never came back!
  They never came back!
  They never came back!
They never came back to me!

EDWARD LEAR

My Mother Said

'My mother said that I never should
Play with the gypsies in the wood,
The wood was dark; the grass was green;
In came Sally with a tambourine.

I went to the sea—no ship to get across;
I paid ten shillings for a blind white horse;
I up on his back and was off in a crack,
Sally, tell my Mother I shall never come back.'

ANONYMOUS

Jacobean Merrymaking

Let the bells ring, and let the boys sing,
    The young lasses skip and play;
Let the cups go round, till round goes the ground,
    Our learned old vicar will stay.

Let the pig turn merrily, merrily, ah,
    And let the fat goose swim;
For verily, verily, verily, ah
    Our vicar this day shall be trim.

The stew'd cock shall crow, cock-a-loodle-loo,
    A loud cock-a-loodle shall he crow;
The duck and the drake shall swim in a lake
    Of onions and claret below.

Our wives shall be neat, to bring in our meat
    To thee our most noble adviser;
Our pains shall be great, and bottles shall sweat,
    And we ourselves will be wiser.

We'll labour and swink, we'll kiss and we'll drink,
    And tithes shall come thicker and thicker;
We'll fall to our plough, and get children enow,
    And thou shalt be learned old vicar.

BEAUMONT AND FLETCHER from *The Spanish Curate*

Swink means to work hard, but can also mean to drink hard. *Tithes* (the tenth part of the produce of the land) were paid to the Vicar of every parish.

83

London Bridge

London Bridge is broken down,
   Dance o'er my lady lee,
London Bridge is broken down,
   With a gay lady.

How shall we build it up again?
   Dance o'er my lady lee,
How shall we build it up again?
   With a gay lady.

Build it up with silver and gold,
   Dance o'er my lady lee,
Build it up with silver and gold,
   With a gay lady.

Silver and gold will be stole away,
   Dance o'er my lady lee,
Silver and gold will be stole away,
   With a gay lady.

Build it up with iron and steel,
   Dance o'er my lady lee,
Build it up with iron and steel,
   With a gay lady.

Iron and steel will bend and bow,
   Dance o'er my lady lee,
Iron and steel will bend and bow,
   With a gay lady.

Build it up with wood and clay,
   Dance o'er my lady lee,
Build it up with wood and clay,
   With a gay lady.

Wood and clay will wash away,
    Dance o'er my lady lee,
Wood and clay will wash away,
    With a gay lady.

Build it up with stone so strong,
    Dance o'er my lady lee,
Huzza! 'twill last for ages long,
    With a gay lady.

ANONYMOUS

I had a Little Nut-tree

I had a little nut-tree, nothing would it bear
But a golden nutmeg and a silver pear;
The King of Spain's daughter came to visit me,
And all for the sake of my little nut-tree.
I skipp'd over water, I danced over sea,
And all the birds in the air couldn't catch me.

ANONYMOUS

She Smiled Like a Holy-day

Sweet she was, as kind a love
  As ever fetter'd swain;
Never such a dainty one
  Shall man enjoy again:
Set a thousand on a row
  I forbid that any show
Ever the like of her,
  Hey nonny nonny noe.

Face she had of filbert hue,
  And bosom'd like a swan;
Back she had of bended yew,
  And waisted by a span.
Hair she had as black as crow
  From the head unto the toe,
Down, down, all over her,
  Hey nonny nonny noe.

She smiled like a holy-day
  And simper'd like the spring;
She prank'd it like a popinjay
  And like a swallow sing;
She trip'd it like a barren doe,
  She strutted like a gor-crow,
Which made the men so fond of her,
  Hey nonny nonny noe.

ANONYMOUS

A *filbert* is a nut. A *popinjay* is a parrot. A *doe* is a female deer. A *gor-crow* is a carrion crow. Swallows do not, strictly speaking, sing; so there is something very like nonsense in the last verse.

Madrigal

My mistress is as fair as fine,
   Milk-white fingers, cherry nose.
Like twinkling day-stars looks her eyne,
   Lightening all things where she goes.
Fair as Phoebe, though not so fickle,
Smooth as glass, though not so brickle.

My heart is as a ball of snow
   Melting at her lukewarm sight;
Her fiery lips like night-worms glow,
   Shining clear as candle-light.
Neat she is, no feather lighter;
Bright she is, no daisy whiter.

THOMAS RAVENSCROFT

It is hard to know whether *cherry nose* is meant to be funny. *Eyne* are eyes.
Brickle is brittle. *Night-worms* are glow-worms.

A Man in the Wilderness

A man in the wilderness asked me,
How many strawberries grow in the sea.
I answered him, as I thought good,
As many red herrings as swim in the wood.

ANONYMOUS

Natural History

What are little boys made of, made of?
What are little boys made of?
   Frogs and snails
   And puppy-dogs' tails,
That's what little boys are made of.

What are little girls made of, made of?
What are little girls made of?
   Sugar and spice
   And all things nice,
That's what little girls are made of.

What are young men made of, made of?
What are young men made of?
   Sighs and leers
   And crocodile tears,
That's what young men are made of.

What are young women made of, made of?
What are young women made of?
   Ribbons and laces
   And sweet pretty faces,
That's what young women are made of.

ANONYMOUS

The Jolly Sixpence

I love sixpence, jolly little sixpence,
  I love sixpence better than my life;
I spent a penny of it, I lent a penny of it,
  And I took fourpence home to my wife.

Oh, my little fourpence, jolly little fourpence,
  I love fourpence better than my life;
I spent a penny of it, I lent a penny of it,
  And I took twopence home to my wife.

Oh, my little twopence, jolly little twopence,
  I love twopence better than my life;
I spent a penny of it, I lent a penny of it,
  And I took nothing home to my wife.

Oh, my little nothing, jolly little nothing,
  What will nothing buy for my wife?
I have nothing, I spend nothing,
  I love nothing better than my wife.

ANONYMOUS

If All the Seas Were One Sea

If all the seas were one sea,
What a *great* sea that would be!
If all the trees were one tree,
What a *great* tree that would be!
And if all the axes were one axe,
What a *great* axe that would be!
And if all the men were one man,
What a *great* man that would be!
And if the *great* man took the *great* axe,
And cut down the *great* tree,
And let it fall into the *great* sea,
What a splish-splash that would be!

ANONYMOUS

Christmas

Christmas is coming,
   The geese are getting fat,
Please to put a penny
   In the old man's hat.
If you haven't got a penny,
   A ha'penny will do;
If you haven't got a ha'penny,
   Then God bless you!

ANONYMOUS

Beautiful Soup

Beautiful Soup, so rich and green,
Waiting in a hot tureen!
Who for such dainties would not stoop?
Soup of the evening, beautiful Soup!
Soup of the evening, beautiful Soup!
   Beau—ootiful Soo—oop!
   Beau—ootiful Soo—oop!
Soo—oop of the e—e—evening,
   Beautiful, beautiful Soup!

Beautiful Soup! Who cares for fish,
Game, or any other dish?
Who would not give all else for two p—
   ennyworth only of beautiful Soup?
Pennyworth only of beautiful Soup?
   Beau—ootiful Soo—oop!
   Beau—ootiful Soo—oop!
Soo—oop of the e—e—evening,
    Beau—ti—ful, beauti—FUL SOUP!

LEWIS CARROLL

Whose Little Pigs?

Whose little pigs are these, these, these?
  Whose little pigs are these?
They are Roger the Cook's, I know by their looks;
  I found them among my peas.
Go pound them, go pound them.
  I dare not on my life,
For though I love not Roger the Cook,
  I dearly love his wife.

ANONYMOUS

To *pound* animals means to put them in a pound—a pen or enclosure.

The Legacy

My father died a month ago
  And left me all his riches;
A feather bed, a wooden leg,
  And a pair of leather breeches;
A coffee pot without a spout,
  A cup without a handle,
A tobacco pipe without a lid,
  And half a farthing candle.

ANONYMOUS

Caution

Mother, may I go out to swim?
   Yes, my darling daughter.
Hang your clothes on a hickory limb
   And don't go near the water.

ANONYMOUS
A *hickory* is a kind of tree.

Queen Anne

Lady Queen Anne she sits in the sun,
As fair as a lily, as white as a swan;
Come taste my lily, come smell my rose,
Which of my maidens do you choose?
The ball is ours and none of yours,
Go to the wood and gather flowers.
Cats and kittens now stay within,
While we young maidens walk out and in.

ANONYMOUS

A Boy's Song

Where the pools are bright and deep,
Where the grey trout lies asleep,
Up the river and over the lea,
That's the way for Billy and me.

Where the blackbird sings the latest,
Where the hawthorn blooms the sweetest,
Where the nestlings chirp and flee,
That's the way for Billy and me.

Where the mowers mow the cleanest,
Where the hay lies thick and greenest,
Where to track the homeward bee,
That's the way for Billy and me.

Where the hazel bank is steepest,
Where the shadow falls the deepest,
Where the clustering nuts fall free,
That's the way for Billy and me.

Why the boys should drive away
Little sweet maidens from the play,
Or love to banter and fight so well,
That's the thing I never could tell.

But this I know, I love to play
Through the meadow, among the hay,
Up the water and over the lea,
That's the way for Billy and me.

JAMES HOGG

96

The Key of the Kingdom

This is the key of the kingdom:
In that kingdom is a city,
In that city is a town,
In that town there is a street,
In that street there winds a lane,
In that lane there is a yard,
In that yard there is a house,
In that house there waits a room,
In that room there is a bed,
On that bed there is a basket,
   A basket full of flowers.

Flowers in the basket,
Basket on the bed,
Bed in the chamber,
Chamber in the house,
House in the weedy yard,
Yard in the winding lane,
Lane in the broad street,
Street in the high town,
Town in the city,
City in the kingdom:
   This is the key of the kingdom.

ANONYMOUS

A Ring Presented to Julia

Julia, I bring
 To thee this ring,
Made for thy finger fit;
 To show by this,
 That our love is
(Or should be) like to it.

 Close though it be,
 The joint is free:
So when Love's yoke is on,
 It must not gall,
 Or fret at all
With hard oppression.

 But it must play
 Still either way;
And be, too, such a yoke,
 As not too wide,
 To over-slide;
Or be so strait to choke.

 So we, who bear,
 This beam, must rear
Ourselves to such a height
 As that the stay
 Of either may
Create the burden light.

 And as this round
 Is nowhere found
To flaw, or else to sever:
 So let our love
 As endless prove;
And pure as gold for ever.

ROBERT HERRICK

The young man gives his girl friend a ring, which (he says) must be like their relationship, free but not too free, and not a burden to them. The two lovers must be like two oxen bearing the wooden yoke for ploughing. *Strait* means narrow. They must both support it equally (the *beam* is the yoke); they must keep it level, so that it is easy to carry. A ring has no end—and their love must be the same.

No Loathsomeness in Love

What I fancy, I approve;
No dislike there is in love :
Be my Mistress short or tall,
And distorted there-withal :
Be she likewise one of those,
That an acre hath of nose :
Be her forehead, and her eyes
Full of incongruities :
Be her cheeks so shallow too,
As to show her tongue wag through;
Be her lips ill hung, or set,
And her grinders black as jet;
Has she thin hair, hath she none,
She's to me a paragon.

ROBERT HERRICK

Incongruities are things that don't go well together. A *paragon* is a perfect person.

The Proposal of Marriage

Sukey, you shall be my wife
    And I will tell you why :
I have got a little pig,
    And you have got a sty;
I have got a dun cow,
    And you can make good cheese;
Sukey, will you marry me ?
    Say Yes, if you please.

ANONYMOUS

Madrigal

Ha ha! ha ha! This world doth pass
  Most merrily I'll be sworn,
For many an honest Indian ass
  Goes for a unicorn.
      Fara diddle dyno,
      This is idle fyno.

Tie hie! tie hie! O sweet delight!
  He tickles this age who can
Call Tullia's ape a marmasyte
  And Leda's goose a swan.
      Fara diddle dyno,
      This is idle fyno.

So so! so so! Fine English days!
  For false play's no reproach,
For he that doth the coachman praise
  May safely use the coach.
      Fara diddle dyno,
      This is idle fyno.

THOMAS WEELKES

A nonsense song, with references to Greek and Latin literature. A
marmazyte is a marmoset (a small monkey). Jupiter visited Leda in the
shape of a swan.

Anacreontic Verse

Brisk methinks I am, and fine,
When I drink my capering wine;
Then to love I do incline,
When I do drink my wanton wine;
And I wish all maidens mine,
When I drink my sprightly wine;
Well I sup, and well I dine,
When I drink my frolic wine;
But I languish, lower, and pine,
When I want my fragrant wine.

ROBERT HERRICK

Anacreon was an Ancient Greek poet who wrote a lot of drinking songs
like this one. *Lower* means to make a frowning face. *Want* means to lack or
be without.

Curly Locks

Curly locks, Curly locks,
   Wilt thou be mine?
Thou shalt not wash dishes
   Nor yet feed the swine;
But sit on a cushion
   And sew a fine seam,
And feed upon strawberries,
   Sugar and cream.

ANONYMOUS

Leaves

Who's killed the leaves?
Me, says the apple, I've killed them all.
Fat as a bomb or a cannonball
I've killed the leaves.

Who sees them drop?
Me, says the pear, they will leave me all bare
So all the people can point and stare.
I see them drop.

Who'll catch their blood?
Me, me, me, says the marrow, the marrow
I'll get so rotund that they'll need a wheelbarrow.
I'll catch their blood.

Who'll make their shroud?
Me, says the swallow, there's just time enough
Before I must pack all my spools and be off.
I'll make their shroud.

Who'll dig their grave?
Me, says the river, with the power of the clouds
A brown deep grave I'll dig under my floods.
I'll dig their grave.

Who'll be their parson?
Me, says the Crow, for it is well-known
I study the bible right down to the bone.
I'll be their parson.

Who'll be chief mourner?
Me, says the wind, I will cry through the grass
The people will pale and go cold when I pass.
I'll be chief mourner.

Who'll carry the coffin?
Me, says the sunset, the whole world will weep
To see me lower it into the deep.
I'll carry the coffin.

Who'll sing a psalm?
Me, says the tractor, with my gear grinding glottle
I'll plough up the stubble and sing through my throttle.
I'll sing the psalm.

Who'll toll the bell?
Me, says the robin, my song in October
Will tell the still gardens the leaves are over.
I'll toll the bell.

TED HUGHES

The Huntsmen

Three jolly gentlemen,
  In coats of red,
Rode their horses
  Up to bed.

Three jolly gentlemen
  Snored till morn,
Their horses champing
  The golden corn.

Three jolly gentlemen,
  At break of day,
Came clitter-clatter down the stairs
  And galloped away.

WALTER DE LA MARE

The Cuckoo

The cuckoo comes in April,
He sings his song in May;
In the middle of June
He changes his tune,
And then he flies away.

Lullaby

Gray goose and gander,
   Waft your wings together,
And carry the good king's daughter
   Over the one-strand river.

Wisdom

For want of a nail
  The shoe was lost,
For want of a shoe
  The horse was lost,
For want of a horse
  The rider was lost,
  For want of a rider
  The battle was lost,
For want of a battle
  The kingdom was lost,
And all for the want
  Of a horse shoe nail.

More Wisdom

A wise old owl sat in an oak,
The more he heard the less he spoke;
The less he spoke the more he heard.
Why aren't we all like that wise old bird?

All these are ANONYMOUS

Love Song

Lavender's blue, diddle, diddle,
   Lavender's green;
When I am king, diddle, diddle,
   You shall be queen.

Who told you so, diddle, diddle,
   Who told you so?
'Twas mine own heart, diddle, diddle,
   That told me so.

Call up your men, diddle, diddle,
   Set them to work,
Some to the plough, diddle, diddle,
   Some to the fork.

Some to make hay, diddle, diddle,
   Some to reap corn,
Whilst you and I, diddle, diddle,
   Keep the bed warm.

Roses are red, diddle, diddle,
   Violets are blue;
Because you love me, diddle, diddle,
   I will love you.

Let the birds sing, diddle, diddle,
   And the lambs play;
We shall be safe, diddle, diddle,
   Out of harm's way.

ANONYMOUS

The Pedlar's Song

When daffodils begin to peer,
   With heigh! the doxy, over the dale,
Why, then comes in the sweet o' the year;
   For the red blood reigns in the winter's pale.

The white sheet bleaching on the hedge,
   With heigh! the sweet birds, O, how they sing!
Doth set my pugging tooth on edge;
   For a quart of ale is a dish for a king.

The lark, that tirra-lirra chants,
   With, heigh! with, heigh! the thrush and the jay,
Are summer songs for me and my aunts,
   While we lie tumbling in the hay.

WILLIAM SHAKESPEARE

This is a song from one of Shakespeare's plays. *Doxy* is a girl-friend,
roughly speaking. So is *aunt*. *Pale* is a boundary. The pedlar was tempted
to steal other people's washing.

Pretty Polly Perkins

Down by the river
Where the green grass grows
Pretty Polly Perkins
   Bleaches her clothes.
She laughs and she sings,
   And she sings so sweet.
She calls, Come over,
   Across the street.
He kissed her, he kissed her,
   He took her to the town;
He bought her a ring
   And a damascene gown.

ANONYMOUS

Damascene is the old name for a kind of material, like damask, a rich silk
cloth with an elaborate patterned design.

The Gunpowder Plot

Please to remember
The Fifth of November,
Gunpowder treason and plot;
I see no reason
Why gunpowder treason
Should ever be forgot.

ANONYMOUS

The Frivolous Cake

A freckled and frivolous cake there was
   That sailed on a pointless sea,
Or any lugubrious lake there was,
   In a manner emphatic and free.
How jointlessly, and how jointlessly
   The frivolous cake sailed by
On the waves of the ocean that pointlessly
   Threw fish to the lilac sky.

Oh, plenty and plenty of hake there was
   Of a glory beyond compare,
And every conceivable make there was
   Was tossed through the lilac air.

Up the smooth billows and over the crests
   Of the cumbersome combers flew
The frivolous cake with a knife in the wake
   Of herself and her curranty crew.
Like a swordfish grim it would bounce and skim
   (This dinner knife fierce and blue),
And the frivolous cake was filled to the brim
   With the fun of her curranty crew.

Oh, plenty and plenty of hake there was
   Of a glory beyond compare—
And every conceivable make there was
   Was tossed through the lilac air.

Around the shores of the Elegant Isles
   Where the cat-fish bask and purr
And lick their paws with adhesive smiles
   And wriggle their fins of fur,
They fly and fly 'neath the lilac sky—
   The frivolous cake, and the knife
Who winketh his glamorous indigo eye
   In the wake of his future wife.

The crumbs blow free down the pointless sea
  To the beat of a cakey heart
And the sensitive steel of the knife can feel
  That love is a race apart.
In the speed of the lingering light are blown
  The crumbs to the hake above,
And the tropical air vibrates to the drone
  Of a cake in the throes of love.

MERVYN PEAKE from: *Titus Groan*

Safe Swimming

Do not fear to put thy feet
Naked in the river, sweet;
Think not leech, or newt, or toad,
Will bite thy foot, when thou hast trod;
Nor let the water rising high,
As thou wad'st in, make thee cry
And sob; but ever live with me,
And not a wave shall trouble thee!

BEAUMONT AND FLETCHER from *The Faithful Shepherdess*

3. ANIMALS

The Owl and the Pussy-Cat

I

The Owl and the Pussy-Cat went to sea
   In a beautiful pea-green boat,
They took some honey, and plenty of money,
   Wrapped up in a five-pound note.
The Owl looked up to the stars above,
   And sang to a small guitar,
'O lovely Pussy! O Pussy, my love,
   'What a beautiful Pussy you are,
      'You are,
      'You are!
   'What a beautiful Pussy you are!'

II

Pussy said to the Owl, 'You elegant fowl!
   'How charmingly sweet you sing!
'O let us be married! too long we have tarried:
   'But what shall we do for a ring?'
They sailed away for a year and a day,
   To the land where the Bong-Tree grows,
And there in a wood a Piggy-wig stood,
   With a ring at the end of his nose,
      His nose,
      His nose,
   With a ring at the end of his nose.

III

'Dear Pig, are you willing to sell for one shilling
   'Your ring?' Said the Piggy, 'I will.'
So they took it away, and were married next day
   By the Turkey who lives on the hill.
They dined on mince, and slices of quince,
   Which they ate with a runcible spoon;
And hand in hand, on the edge of the sand,
   They danced by the light of the moon,
      The moon,
      The moon,
   They danced by the light of the moon.

EDWARD LEAR

The Ferret

There is one animal of merit
And perfect honesty: the Ferret.

I have not time to tell to you
The numerous things that he will do.

For if you do not overtask him,
He will do anything you ask him.

He is as clever as a pike,
He will do anything you like.

He is as faithful as a bear,
And gentle as a Belgian hare.

He is as strong as any fish,
He will do anything you wish:

Bite holes in leaves, tie knots in string,
Or practically anything.

LORD ALFRED DOUGLAS

The Python

A Python I should not advise,—
It needs a doctor for its eyes,
   And has the measles yearly.

However, if you feel inclined
To get one (to improve your mind,
   And not from fashion merely),
Allow no music near its cage;
And when it flies into a rage
   Chastise it most severely.

I had an Aunt in Yucatan
Who bought a Python from a man
   And kept it for a pet.
She died because she never knew
These simple little rules and few;—
   The snake is living yet.

HILAIRE BELLOC

To the Bat

Bat, bat, come under my hat,
   And I'll give you a slice of bacon;
And when I bake, I'll give you a cake,
   If I am not mistaken.

ANONYMOUS

Leaving School

Our Blackheath Comprehensive School (for mice)
Provides a master who will give advice
About careers; and if he's not a fool,
In his last term, or earlier, at school
A mouse should see this master on the tricky
Problem of work. His name is Mr Michie.
His desk is covered with brochures on what
Sheer fun it is to join the Army, not
A cat in sight, while you, sent overseas,
Chat up the local ladies over cheese;
On openings in Town (where jobs abound
And even humans travel underground).
Perhaps the most attractive are the places
Where the top portion of the human race is—
Those vacancies for clearing up the bits
In the vast kitchens of the hotel Ritz
Or the Elysium of the hungry mouse—
After a garden party at Buck House,
Where every woman (also every man)
Leave their Swiss Rolls to gawp at Princess Anne.
Of course, few rodents have the *savoir faire*
To keep up with the social standards there—
Not to neglect to bow, say, to the Prince,
Hiding your tart of strawberry jam or mince.

So Michie, talking to a rather hairy
School-leaver called (you might have guessed it) Gary,
Advised against the Piccadilly scene
And also lodging with HM the Queen.
'Gary,' he said, 'I'd like to see you try
For something in science or technology.
One of the Defence Establishments, perhaps,
Working on antidotes and anti-traps.'

'Oh no, sir. Such things aren't for me. I've planned
To tour the world with what you'd call my "band"'—
In fact a group known as "The Bacon Rind."'

'Ah Gary, I'm afraid you're just as blind
As those Three of our species in the rhyme.
At least a million young mice at this time
Aspire to make a journey to the stars
By beating drums or strumming on guitars.
And all they do is prove what people say—
"As noisy as a mouse." Mice shouldn't play
If the (rock) cats are going to stay away.'

'Oh very clever, sir. But I'm a mouse
Already booked for TV's *Second House.*
Fame among highbrows will be in the bag
After we're introduced by Melvyn Bragg.'

ROY FULLER

Parrot

Sometimes I sit with both eyes closed,
But all the same, I've heard!
They're saying, 'He won't talk because
He is a *thinking* bird.'

I'm olive-green and sulky, and
The family say, 'Oh yes,
He's silent, but he's *listening*,
He *thinks* more than he *says*!

'He ponders on the things he hears,
Preferring not to chatter.'
—And this is true, but *why* it's true
Is quite another matter.

I'm working out some shocking things
In order to surprise them,
And when my thoughts are ready I'll
Certainly *not* disguise them!

I'll wait, and see, and choose a time
When everyone is present,
And clear my throat and raise my beak
And give a squawk and start to speak
And go on for about a week
And it will not be pleasant!

ALAN BROWNJOHN

Any Part of Piggy

Any part of piggy
Is quite all right with me
Ham from Westphalia, ham from Parma
Ham as lean as the Dalai Lama
Ham from Virginia, ham from York,
Trotters, sausages, hot roast pork.
Crackling crisp for my teeth to grind on
Bacon with or without the rind on
Though humanitarian
I'm not a vegetarian.
I'm neither crank nor prude nor prig
And though it may sound infra dig
Any part of darling pig
Is perfectly fine with me.

NOEL COWARD

The Ibis

The Ibis
Is born believing that his tribe is
Sacred upon the Nile;
Whereas, for a long while,
It most decidedly has not
Been too sacred to be shot,
Though it remains sacred enough
To stuff.
Parents hasten to describe this
Danger to the infant Ibis.

MARIE DE L. WELCH

Hi!

Hi! handsome hunting man,
Fire your little gun.
Bang! Now the animal
Is dead and dumb and done.
Never more to peep again, creep again, leap again,
Eat or sleep or drink again. Oh, what fun!

WALTER DE LA MARE

The Lion and the Unicorn

The lion and the unicorn,
    Fighting for the crown,
The lion beat the unicorn
    All thro' the town,
And when he had beat him out,
    He beat him in again;
He beat him three times over,
    His power to maintain.

ANONYMOUS

124

The Crocodile

Whatever our faults, we can always engage
That no fancy or fable shall sully our page,
  So take note of what follows, I beg.
This creature so grand and august in its age,
  In its youth is hatched out of an egg.

    And oft in some far Coptic town
    The Missionary sits him down
      To breakfast by the Nile:
    The heart beneath his priestly gown
      Is innocent of guile;
    When suddenly the rigid frown
    Of Panic is observed to drown
      His customary smile.

    Why does he start and leap amain,
    And scour the sandy Libyan plain
    Like one that wants to catch a train,
    Or wrestles with internal pain?
    Because he finds his egg contain—
    Green, hungry, horrible and plain—
      An Infant Crocodile.

HILAIRE BELLOC

Kindness

I love little pussy,
  Her coat is so warm,
And if I don't hurt her
  She'll do me no harm.
So I'll not pull her tail,
  Nor drive her away,
But pussy and I
  Very gently will play.
She shall sit by my side,
  And I'll give her some food;
And pussy will love me
  Because I am good.

ANONYMOUS

The Frog

Be kind and tender to the Frog,
  And do not call him names,
As 'Slimy skin', or 'Polly-wog,'
  Or likewise 'Ugly James,'
Or 'Gap-a-grin,' or 'Toad-gone-wrong,'
  Or 'Billy Bandy-knees':
The Frog is justly sensitive
  To epithets like these.
No animal will more repay
  A treatment kind and fair;
At least so lonely people say
Who keep a frog (and, by the way,
  They are extremely rare).

HILAIRE BELLOC

Elephant

It is quite unfair to be
obliged to be so large, so I suppose
you could call me discontented.

Think big, they said, when
I was a little elephant; they
wanted to get me used to it.

It was kind. But it doesn't help if,
inside, you are carefree in small ways,
fond of little amusements.

You are smaller than me, think
how conveniently near the flowers are,
how you can pat the cat by just

halfbending over. You can also
arrange teacups for dolls, play
marbles in the proper season.

I would give anything to be
able to do a tiny, airy, flitting
dance to show how very little a

thing happiness can be really.

ALAN BROWNJOHN

The Hippopotamus

I shoot the Hippopotamus with bullets made of platinum,
Because if I use leaden ones his hide is sure to flatten 'em.

HILAIRE BELLOC

The Ostrich

The Ostrich always seems to try
If he can peck you in the eye.

And if he can't succeed in that,
He gives a kick and knocks you flat.

And when he's rolled you in the mud,
He eats your flesh and laps your blood.

About this bird there's one good thing,—
He never hits you with his wing.

And he is very easily pleased
When once his appetite's appeased.

LORD ALFRED DOUGLAS

The Weasel

The Weasel is a perfect dear,
He'll never give you cause to fear.

If you walk out on a fine day,
He bounds before you all the way.

And if your boots are rather tight,
He bites them till they fit all right.

LORD ALFRED DOUGLAS

The Lion and the Unicorn
(Another Version)

The lion and the unicorn
   Were fighting for the crown;
The lion beat the unicorn
   All around the town.

Some gave them white bread,
   And some gave them brown;
Some gave them plum cake
   And drummed them out of town.

ANONYMOUS

4. PEOPLE

The Milkmaid

Where are you going to, my pretty maid?
I'm going a-milking, sir, she said,
Sir, she said, sir, she said,
I'm going a-milking, sir, she said.

May I go with you, my pretty maid?
You're kindly welcome, sir, she said,
Sir, she said, sir, she said,
You're kindly welcome, sir, she said.

Say, will you marry me, my pretty maid?
Yes, if you please, kind sir, she said,
Sir, she said, sir, she said,
Yes, if you please, kind sir, she said.

What is your father, my pretty maid?
My father's a farmer, sir, she said,
Sir, she said, sir, she said,
My father's a farmer, sir, she said.

What is your fortune, my pretty maid?
My face is my fortune, sir, she said,
Sir, she said, sir, she said,
My face is my fortune, sir, she said.

Then I can't marry you, my pretty maid.
Nobody asked you, sir, she said,
Sir, she said, sir, she said,
Nobody asked you, sir, she said.

ANONYMOUS

A Butcher

Whoe'er has gone thro' London Street,
Has seen a Butcher gazing at his
    meat
    And how he keeps
    Gloating upon a sheep's
Or bullock's personals, as if his own;
    How he admires his halves
    And quarters—and his calves,
As if in truth upon his own legs grown;—
    His fat! his suet!
His kidneys peeping elegantly thro' it!
    His thick flank!
    And his thin!
      His shank!
      His shin!
Skin of his skin, and bone too of his
    bone!

    With what an air
He stands aloof, across the thorough-
    fare
Gazing—and will not let a body by,
Tho' buy! buy! buy! be constantly
    his cry.
Meanwhile with arms a-kimbo, and a pair
Of Rhodian legs he revels in a stare
At his Joint Stock—for one may call
    it so,
    Howbeit, without a Co.
The dotage of self-love was never
    fonder
Than he of his brute bodies all a-row;
Narcissus in the wave did never ponder
    With love so strong,
    On his 'portrait charmant'
As our vain Butcher on his carcase
    yonder.

Look at his sleek round skull!
How bright his cheek, how rubicund
   his nose is!
His visage seems to be
   Ripe for beef-tea;
Of brutal juices the whole man is
   full.—
In fact, fulfilling the metempsychosis,
The Butcher is already half a Bull.

THOMAS HOOD

The Butcher's legs are called *Rhodian* because they are very big. A gigantic statue, the Colossus, used to be the pride of Rhodes, and of the Ancient World. *Metempsychosis* is the idea that people's souls can be transferred to animals.

Byways in Biography

Alfred de Musset
Used to call his cat Pusset.
His accent was affected.
That was to be expected.

MAURICE HARE

Trial and Error

A lady is smarter than a gentleman, maybe.
She can sew a fine seam, she can have a baby,
She can use her intuition instead of her brain,
But she can't fold a paper on a crowded train.

PHYLLIS MCGINLEY

The Miller of Dee

There was a jolly miller once,
    Lived on the river Dee;
He worked and sang from morn till night,
    No lark more blithe than he.
And this the burden of his song
    Forever used to be,
I care for nobody, no! not I,
    If nobody cares for me.

ANONYMOUS

138

Henry King

Who chewed bits of String, and was early cut off in Dreadful Agonies.

The Chief Defect of Henry King
Was chewing little bits of String.
At last he swallowed some which tied
Itself in ugly Knots inside.

Physicians of the Utmost Fame
Were called at once; but when they came
They answered, as they took their Fees,
'There is no Cure for this Disease.
Henry will very soon be dead.'
His Parents stood about his Bed
Lamenting his Untimely Death,
When Henry, with his Latest Breath,
Cried—'Oh, my Friends, be warned by me,
That Breakfast, Dinner, Lunch and Tea
Are all the Human Frame requires . . .'
With that, the Wretched Child expires.

HILAIRE BELLOC

Pooh!

Dainty Miss Apathy
Sat on a sofa,
Dangling her legs,
And with nothing to do;
She looked at a drawing of
Old Queen Victoria,
At a rug from far Persia—
An exquisite blue;
At a bowl of bright tulips;
A needlework picture
Of doves caged in wicker
You could almost hear coo;
She looked at the switch
That evokes e-
Lectricity;
At the coals of an age
B.C. millions and two—
When the trees were like ferns
And the reptiles all flew;
She looked at the cat
Asleep on the hearthrug,
At the sky at the window,—
The clouds in it, too;
And a marvellous light
From the West burning through:
And the one silly word
In her desolate noddle
As she dangled her legs,
Having nothing to do,
Was not, as you'd guess,
Of dumfoundered felicity,
But contained just four letters,
And these pronounced *Pooh!*

WALTER DE LA MARE

Apathy means not being interested. Miss Apathy was simply bored.

140

The Rival Curates

List while the poet trolls
  Of MR CLAYTON HOOPER,
Who had a cure of souls
  At Spiffton-extra-Sooper.

He lived on curds and whey,
  And daily sang their praises,
And then he'd go and play
  With buttercups and daisies.

Wild croquet HOOPER banned,
  And all the sports of Mammon,
He warred with cribbage, and
  He exorcized backgammon.

His helmet was a glance
  That spoke of holy gladness;
A saintly smile his lance;
  His shield a tear of sadness.

His Vicar smiled to see
  This armour on him buckled;
With pardonable glee
  He blessed himself and chuckled.

'In mildness to abound
  My curate's sole design is;
In all the country round
  There's none so mild as mine is!'

And HOOPER, disinclined
  His trumpet to be blowing,
Yet didn't think you'd find
  A milder curate going.

A friend arrived one day
  At Spiffton-extra-Sooper,
And in this shameful way
  He spoke to MR HOOPER:

'You think your famous name
　For mildness can't be shaken,
That none can blot your fame—
　But, HOOPER, you're mistaken!

'Your mind is not as blank
　As that of HOPLEY PORTER,
Who holds a curate's rank
　As Assesmilk-cum-Worter.

'*He* plays the airy flute,
　And looks depressed and blighted,
Doves round about him "toot",
　And lambkins dance delighted.

'*He* labours more than you
　At worsted work, and frames it;
In old maids' albums, too,
　Sticks seaweed—yes, and names it!'

The tempter said his say,
　Which pierced him like a needle—
He summoned straight away
　His sexton and his beadle.

(These men were men who could
　Hold liberal opinions:
On Sundays they were good—
　On week-days they were minions.)

'To HOPLEY PORTER go,
　Your fare I will afford you—
Deal him a deadly blow,
　And blessings shall reward you.

'But stay—I do not like
　Undue assassination,
And so, before you strike,
　Make this communication:

'I'll give him this one chance—
  If he'll more gaily bear him,
Play croquet, smoke, and dance,
  I willingly will spare him.'

They went, those minions true,
  To Assesmilk-cum-Worter,
And told their errand to
  The REVEREND HOPLEY PORTER.

'What?' said that reverend gent,
  'Dance through my hours of leisure?
Smoke?—bathe myself with scent?—
  Play croquet? Oh, with pleasure!

'Wear all my hair in curl?
  Stand at my door, and wink—so—
At every passing girl?
  My brothers, I should think so!

W. S. GILBERT

Mammon was a heathen god. *Cribbage* is a card game. *Backgammon* is
played with draughts and dice. *Sextons* and *beadles* are Church officials.

Solomon Grundy

Solomon Grundy,
Born on a Monday,
Christened on Tuesday,
Married on Wednesday,
Took ill on Thursday,
Worse on Friday,
Died on Saturday,
Buried on Sunday.
This is the end
Of Solomon Grundy.

ANONYMOUS

Miss T.

It's a very odd thing—
    As odd as can be—
That whatever Miss T. eats
    Turns into Miss T.;
Porridge and apples,
    Mince, muffins and mutton,
Jam, junket, jumbles—
    Not a rap, not a button
It matters; the moment
    They're out of her plate,
Though shared by Miss Butcher
    And sour Miss Bate;
Tiny and cheerful,
    And neat as can be,
Whatever Miss T. eats
    Turns into Miss T.

WALTER DE LA MARE

The Weather

What's the weather on about?
Why is the rain so down on us?
Why does the sun glare at us so?

Why does the hail dance so prettily?
Why is the snow such an overall?
Why is the wind such a tearaway?

Why is the mud so fond of our feet?
Why is the ice so keen to upset us?
Who does the weather think it is?

GAVIN EWART

A Nocturnal Sketch

Even is come; and from the dark Park, hark,
The signal of the setting sun—one gun!
And six is sounding from the chime, prime time
To go and see the Drury-Lane Dane slain,—
Or hear Othello's jealous doubt spout out,—
Or Macbeth raving at that shade-made blade,
Denying to his frantic clutch much touch;—
Or else to see Ducrow with wide stride ride
Four horses as no other man can span;
Or in the small Olympic Pit, sit split
Laughing at Liston, while you quiz his phiz.
Anon Night comes, and with her wings brings things
Such as with his poetic tongue, Young sung;
The gas up-blazes with its bright white light,
And paralytic watchmen prowl, howl, growl,
About the streets and take up Pall-Mall Sal,
Who, hasting to her nightly jobs, robs fobs.

Now thieves to enter for your cash, smash, crash,
Past drowsy Charley, in a deep sleep, creep,
But frightened by Policeman B3, flee,
And while they're going, whisper low, 'No go!'
Now puss, while folks are in their beds, treads leads,
And sleepers waking, grumble—'Drat that cat!'
Who in the gutter catterwauls, squalls, mauls
Some feline foe, and screams in shrill ill-will.

Now Bulls of Bashan, of a prize size, rise
In childish dreams, and with a roar gore poor
Georgy or Charley, or Billy, willy-nilly;—
But Nursemaid, in a nightmare rest, chest-pressed,
Dreameth of one of her old flames, James Games,
And that she hears—what faith is man's!—Ann's banns
And his, from Reverend Mr. Rice, twice, thrice:
White ribbons flourish, and a stout shout out,
That upward goes, shows Rose know those bows' woes!

THOMAS HOOD

This is London in 1840 or so. The *Drury-Lane Dane* is Hamlet. *Quiz* is
slang for 'to look at'. *Phiz* is face. *Liston* was a comic actor. *Young* was a
famous English poet who wrote 'Night Thoughts'. *Fobs* are watch-
pockets. *Bulls of Bashan* occur in the Bible. *Rose*, a nursemaid, dreams her
boy friend James (probably a footman) is marrying her friend Ann.

As it Fell Upon a Day

Oh! what's befallen Bessy Brown,
  She stands so squalling in the street;
She's let her pitcher tumble down,
  And all the water's at her feet!

The little schoolboys stood about,
  And laughed to see her pumping, pumping;
Now with a curtsey to the spout,
  And then upon her tiptoes jumping.

Long time she waited for her neighbours
  To have their turns:—but she must lose
The watery wages of her labours,—
  Except a little in her shoes!

Without a voice to tell her tale,
  And ugly transport in her face;
All like a jugless nightingale,
  She thinks of her bereaved case.

At last she sobs—she cries—she screams!—
  And pours her flood of sorrows out,
From eyes and mouth, in mingled streams,
  Just like the lion on the spout.

For well poor Bessy knows her mother
  Must lose her tea, for water's lack,
That Sukey burns—and baby-brother
  Must be dry-rubbed with huck-a-back!

THOMAS HOOD

As it fell upon a day is an old phrase used in telling stories (= as it
happened one day). Here there is a pun on the fact that Bessy's jug *fell*.
Transport means passion. She is lamenting, like the nightingale, but not
making the *jug-jug* noise that nightingales are supposed to make. In
London, as well as the country, water came from pumps, often with a
lion's head for a mouth. Because there is no water her little brother will
have to be cleaned with a dry towel (*huck-a-back* is a towelling material).
Why Sukey should burn, I have no idea.

Bad Sir Brian Botany

Sir Brian had a battleaxe with great big knobs on;
He went among the villagers and blipped them on the head.
On Wednesday and on Saturday, but mostly on the latter
 day,
He called at all the cottages, and this is what he said:
  'I am Sir Brian!' (ting-ling)
  'I am Sir Brian!' (rat-tat)
  'I am Sir Brian, as bold as a lion—
  Take *that*!—and *that*!—and *that*!'

Sir Brian had a pair of boots with great big spurs on,
A fighting pair of which he was particularly fond.
On Tuesday and on Friday, just to make the street look tidy,
He'd collect the passing villagers and kick them in the pond.
  'I am Sir Brian!' (sper-lash!)
  'I am Sir Brian!' (sper-losh!)
  'I am Sir Brian, as bold as a lion—
  Is anyone else for a wash?'

Sir Brian woke one morning, and he couldn't find his
 battleaxe;
He walked into the village in his second pair of boots.
He had gone a hundred paces, when the street was full of
 faces,
And the villagers were round him with ironical salutes,
  'You are Sir Brian? Indeed!
  You are Sir Brian? Dear, dear!
  You are Sir Brian, as bold as a lion?
  Delighted to meet you here!'

Sir Brian went a journey, and he found a lot of duckweed:
They pulled him out and dried him, and they blipped him
 on the head.
They took him by the breeches, and they hurled him into
 ditches,

And they pushed him under waterfalls, and this is what they
  said:
    'You are Sir Brian—don't laugh,
    You are Sir Brian—don't cry;
    You are Sir Brian, as bold as a lion—
    Sir Brian, the lion, good-bye!

Sir Brian struggled home again, and chopped up his
  battleaxe,
Sir Brian took his fighting boots, and threw them in the fire.
He is quite a different person now he hasn't got his spurs on,
And he goes about the village as B. Botany, Esquire.
    'I am Sir Brian? Oh, *no!*
    I am Sir Brian? Who's he?
    I haven't got any title, I'm Botany—
    Plain Mr. Botany (B).'

A. A. MILNE

Domestic Asides;

or, Truth in Parentheses

'I really take it very kind,
This visit, Mrs. Skinner!
I have not seen you such an age—
(The wretch has come to dinner!)

'Your daughters, too, what loves of girls—
What heads for painters' easels!
Come here and kiss the infant, dears—
(And give it p'rhaps the measles!)

'Your charming boys I see are home
From Reverend Mr. Russell's;
'Twas very kind to bring them both—
(What boots for my new Brussels!)

'What! little Clara left at home?
Well now I call that shabby:
I should have loved to kiss her so—
(A flabby, dabby, babby!)

'And Mr. S., I hope he's well,
Ah! though he lives so handy,
He never now drops in to sup—
(The better for our brandy!)

'Come, take a seat—I long to hear
About Matilda's marriage;
You're come of course to spend the day!
(Thank Heaven, I hear the carriage!)

'What! Must you go? next time I hope
You'll give me longer measure;
Nay—I shall see you down the stairs—
(With most uncommon pleasure!)

'Good-bye! good-bye! remember all,
Next time you'll take your dinners!
(Now, David, mind I'm not at home
In future to the Skinners!)

THOMAS HOOD

This poem is spoken by a lady who has been unexpectedly visited by a
family she does not much like. Her real thoughts are in parentheses
(brackets, like this). Her *'new Brussels'* is a carpet. In the last two lines she
tells her servant David to say she is *not at home* if they call again.

Old Woman of Croydon

There was an Old Woman of Croydon,
To look young she affected the Hoyden,
And would jump and would skip,
Till she put out her hip;
Alas poor Old Woman of Croydon.

ANONYMOUS (1820)

There was once a man of Bengal,
Who was asked to a fancy dress ball;
He murmured 'I'll risk it,
And go as a biscuit';
But a dog ate him up in the hall.

ANONYMOUS

There was a faith healer of Deal,
Who said 'Although pain isn't real,
If I sit on a pin
And it punctures my skin,
I dislike what I fancy I feel.'

ANONYMOUS

There was a young lady of Ryde,
Who ate some green apples and died;
The apples fermented
Inside the lamented
And made cider inside her inside.

ANONYMOUS

There was once a pious young priest
Who lived almost wholly on yeast,
'For' he said 'it is plain
We must all rise again,
And I want to get started at least.'

ANONYMOUS

Epigram

Sir, I admit your general rule,
That every poet is a fool:
But you yourself may serve to show it,
That every fool is not a poet.

MATTHEW PRIOR

The Jungle Husband

Dearest Evelyn, I often think of you
Out with the guns in the jungle stew
Yesterday I hittapotamus
I put the measurements down for you but they got lost in the
    fuss
It's not a good thing to drink out here
You know, I've practically given it up dear.
Tomorrow I am going alone a long way
Into the jungle. It is all grey
But green on top
Only sometimes when a tree has fallen
The sun comes down plop, it is quite appalling.
You never want to go in a jungle pool
In the hot sun, it would be the act of a fool
Because it's always full of anacondas, Evelyn, not looking ill-
    fed
I'll say. So no more now, from your loving husband,
    Wilfred.

STEVIE SMITH

Traditional People

Lack Wit

When I was a little boy
   I had but little wit;
'Tis a long time ago,
   And I have no more yet;
Nor ever, ever shall,
   Until that I die,
For the longer I live
   The more fool am I.

Jerry Hall

Jerry Hall,
He is so small,
A rat could eat him,
Hat and all.

Sulky Sue

Here's Sulky Sue;
What shall we do?
Turn her face to the wall
Till she comes to.

Cross-Patch

Cross-Patch,
Draw the latch,
Sit by the fire and spin;
Take a cup
And drink it up,
Then call your neighbours in.

Robin and Richard

Robin and Richard
Were two pretty men,
They lay in bed
Till the clock struck ten;
Then up starts Robin
And looks at the sky,
Oh, brother Richard,
The sun's very high.
You go before
With bottle and bag,
And I will come after
On little Jack Nag.

Elsie Marley

Elsie Marley is grown so fine,
She won't get up to feed the swine,
But lies in bed till eight or nine.
Lazy Elsie Marley!

A Grenadier

Who comes here?
  A grenadier.
What do you want?
  A pot of beer.
Where's your money?
  I forgot it.
Get you gone,
  You silly blockhead.

My Mammy's Maid

Dingty diddlety,
  My mammy's maid,
She stole oranges,
  I am afraid;
Some in her pocket,
  Some in her sleeve,
She stole oranges,
  I do believe.

Doctor Fell

I do not like thee, Doctor Fell,
The reason why I cannot tell;
But this I know, and know full well,
I do not like thee, Doctor Fell.